THE CURRENCY OF THE FUTURE

*When You Know This,
You Control Your Destiny.*

BRAD DEHAVEN

ISBN 0-9722332-3-7

Published by MotiVision Media

FIRST EDITION March 2005

Content Editor and Writer–Naomi Goegan
Cover Design–MotiVision Media
Layout and Graphics–MotiVision Media

Special thanks to the following people for their contribution on this project: Scott Michael, Kim DeHaven, Lynn Ehrenburg, Chris Goegan, Denise Stephens, John Cordova, Ernie Goyette, and my three children: Blake, Bailey, and Brady.
To Naomi: You are gifted and I am blessed. Thank you!

I thank all the leaders who have impacted my life through their example.

"When a strong man takes a stand, the spines of others are stiffened."

Contents

THE CURRENCY OF THE FUTURE

Forward

Do something great with your life

D o you remember what you dreamed about as a kid? Did you ever think of becoming an astronaut, a movie star, or even the President of the United States? I know I did. As a kid I was a great athlete, a hard worker, and a big dreamer. Maybe I would be a professional surfer, or perhaps a big business leader. I always felt that I was meant to do something great with my life. One of my big dreams was to someday be an NFL superstar like my dad, who played for the Dallas Cowboys under Tom Landry.

It was that dream I envisioned that carried me through the grueling two-a-day football practices in high school. Why else would I have chosen to wake up at 6 a.m. and run up and down stadium steps in the scorching August heat? I'll never forget the feeling of my calves burning and the sound of those steel bleachers chattering under my cleated feet. No wonder they called it "hell week"! It was sheer agony, but inside of me I knew I wanted to perform for my dad, for the team, and to set a great example. I wanted to stand out in the crowd and be a winner. The dream of victory is what kept me going.

I can picture it as clear as day. The stands are full of wildly cheering fans, the band's drums echoing in the night as our team gathers for one last pep talk before bursting onto the field. We play our hearts out through blood, sweat, and tears, and the game is close, but we come out of it victorious! Haven't you ever had dreams like that? I never did become an NFL superstar, but thanks to the great cheerleaders who encouraged me along the way, I have been fortunate enough to see some of my dreams come true in my life. How about you? Well, I'm here to let you know that you can do it! There's a giant inside each and every one of us–yes, *you* too! And when that giant awakens–watch out! Miracles happen.

I remember a business trip I took to Oakland once. After being away from my wife and kids for a few days, I was anxious to get home so I arrived at my departing gate early. I settled into a chair and pulled out a book when out of the corner of my eye, I caught a glimpse of a gentleman whose briefcase had spilled out onto the floor. I jumped up to help him and we exchanged a few words and a handshake. His name was George. As he gathered his things and began to head off, something came over me and I called out to him, "George!" He stopped and turned around to look at me. "Do something *great* with your life." There was an awkward silence and it was as if he and I were the only ones standing in that terminal. He thought for a moment, smiled, and turned to go. I sat back down and started reading my book again when I noticed someone walking up to me. It was George. "Brad," he said with a tear running down one cheek, "I'm 64 years old and no one has ever told me that. Thank you, thank you."

You see, I know you can do something great with your life. I believe we all have the capacity to live our best life. Why not join me on an adventure? Be bold and take a chance on you. I think you'll discover that your greatest moments lay ahead of you in *The Currency of the Future*.

Brad DeHaven

Chapter I
The Winds of Change

What is The Currency of the Future? Is it a promising dot com or stock market strategy? A high IQ, good grades, and a college diploma? Or, is it just a lucky break that happens to a fortunate few? Remember that old phrase, "A penny for your thoughts?" The Currency of the Future states, "I'll bet a million on your capacity to think!" This book is based on the premise that you contain the magic to do great things with your life. I believe that somewhere buried within every one of us is an idealist looking to make an impact in a big way. Discover your ability to think and act, and you will. The life you've only imagined until now is waiting for you to step up to the plate and create it. You're sitting on a gold mine and it's time you started cashing in on it.

Never before has there been a better time for you to make your move. The winds of change are in your favor. Right here and now is your chance to follow your passions, make your mark, and own your one and only life. You may be thinking, "Yeah, yeah, I've heard it all before." Then it's time to start listening, absorbing, and acting because the only thing standing between you and the fortune that you're worth is the six inches between your ears. *You* are The Currency of the Future. Your thinking and your actions are what determine your life. Stop the

1

noise for a moment and tell me–are you ready? Will you join me in the greatest discovery of your life? If your answer is yes, then we're ready to talk about your future. If your answer is no, then it's time to wake up and face the truth about your life: You only get one. So why not live a great one? It's not a fire-drill or a practice-run. You don't get a second chance!

When you blow it on an X-Box game you can press the "restart" button. When you mess up on a spreadsheet you can just open a new file. But in life, you don't have that option. You are only going to live your life once.

Are you having fun? Are you making what you're worth? Are you making a difference? Be honest. There's no one watching you read this book right now. It's just you and me. What does your heart tell you?

These aren't small questions are they? They'll shake you up a bit if you really ponder them. If your heart says, "No, no, and no." Here's the good news: The times in our lives that we feel we have the least power are actually the times when we have the most. These are the times when we decide to act, to redefine who we are, what we believe, and make the significant decisions that alter our destiny.

Let me tell you what we're going to cover in this book. First, we're going to take a look at some business and social trends that are affecting the way we work. We'll discuss why now, more than ever, we must consider change and how we can profit from it. Next, we'll talk about some of the fundamental skills and attitudes you'll need to capitalize on the opportunities of the future. Then finally, we're going to throw some fuel behind it all to get you up to high gear and give you the greatest chance for success.

"The significant problems we face in life cannot be solved by the same level of thinking that created them." –Albert Einstein

Engine Check

Before we step on the gas, let's make sure your engine's really ready for the undertaking. Take a minute and ask yourself honestly–how do

THE CURRENCY OF THE FUTURE

"The only thing standing between you and the fortune that you're worth is the 6 inches between your ears."

–Brad DeHaven

you rate from 1 to 10 in the following two areas. 1 being the least and 10 being the most:

How **Teachable** are you? Do you ask a lot of questions and try to gain information whenever possible, or are you a "know it all"? Do you dish out your opinion about most things, or do you find yourself searching for answers? Are you typically the one doing the talking or the listening? Rate yourself now for how teachable you are. _____

How **Motivated** are you? If you got swept up in a great idea, would you perform? Are you eager to change to get what you want? Do you find yourself avoiding change at all cost, or do you invite it? Are you typically open to new ideas, or do your fences come up? Do you value comfort and acceptance over progress? Give yourself a higher number if people would describe you as ambitious and self-motivated. If you resist new things and goal setting, give yourself a lower number. Rate yourself now for how motivated you are. _____

Now take those two numbers and multiply them together. You will have a number somewhere between 0 and 100. Let's see where you are:

70–100　　Congratulations! You will get tons of value from this book.
50–69　　You can expect good results.
30–49　　This book can make a noticeable difference.
0–30　　　I would challenge you with this: Could there be something you can think of that would actually motivate you to change? If so, stay with me; a change can be the most exciting thing that ever happened to you. If you really can't think of anything that will motivate you, take this book back and exchange it for a novel or go watch TV.

Here's why these two qualities (teachable & motivated) are critical. This book isn't just a bunch of information about trends or business success. Information requires no response, no reaction, and no results. Rather, it is a book of instructions, which, if digested and acted upon, will change your life forever. We've heard that "Knowledge is power." In reality–"Applied knowledge is power." Action in agreement with great instruction is the crux of progress.

THE CURRENCY OF THE FUTURE

"A period of great change
is the 'best of times' for those
who have the vision to profit
by new economic arrangements
and the 'worst of times' for those
who continue to rely on old
crumbling institutions."
–William Stanmeyer

Okay, one last thing. Most journeys begin by packing a suitcase, this one will not. The journey into The Currency of the Future requires you to dump the baggage now. Whatever you're carrying with you from the past–lose it. Give yourself a fighting chance and start fresh without the junk. Go ahead and leave the past behind.

> Past disappointments
> Past failures
> Past mistakes
> Past attitudes
> Past beliefs

My friend John always says, "Give up on the hope of a better past." You can't bring your same old self into a bright new future. Success requires change, growth, and a fresh outlook on your life's journey. Bury your past or your past will bury you. Do it now; get rid of that dead weight holding you back and look forward to the adventure ahead. *Now*, we're ready to go!

A Period of Great Change
Let's face it, times are changing and technology is moving at warp speed. Gone are the days when it was possible to start working at eighteen and retire from that same industry forty or fifty years later. The world is changing to a global economy and our thinking needs to adapt and evolve along with it.

Our society is about to witness an explosion in non-conventional ways to answer the basic economic question: ***"How do I make a good living?"*** The next decade will reveal a tidal wave of opportunities through technology in home-managed professions enabled by mobile devices and increasing efficiencies of the web. The trends are moving away from mass employment and new opportunities coupled with the web are blowing the traditional job paradigm to pieces. More and more people are breaking free from the chains of earning a living. Rather than clinging to job security and living paycheck to paycheck, workers are exploring new and better ways to build a life on their terms.

Web designers, freelance writers, accountants, and countless other professionals today, both self-employed and full payroll, are performing their 9 to 5 in their PJs. They are capable of working from just about anywhere: while sipping on a vanilla latte at the neighborhood Starbucks, flying over the Pacific at 35,000 feet, or sitting in the courtesy lounge while waiting for an oil-change. These new professionals have technology to thank, and its conveniences are just now beginning to take hold in the workplace.

The web has revolutionized the way the world does life and business. Yet, if we think of the possibilities, its impact on society is still in its infancy. Think about it: The Internet came into public use in the mid 90s and ten years later, business over the Internet accounts for over $100 billion annually! The changes to come are absolutely staggering. Here's an amazing fact: 80 percent of the technology we will use in our day-to-day lives 10 years from now has not even been invented yet. Imagine that! Due to the pace of technology, a trillion dollars of business is moving from brick and mortar stores to click and order over the Internet and the Web is rapidly becoming the infrastructure of the new economy.

Blindsided!

A friend of mine introduced me to Jim Harris, author of a book titled *Blindsided*. In his book, Jim talks about several companies that have been blindsided by the recent changes in technology. Let me share a few of his examples with you:

> *In 1999, an 18 year old kid named Shawn Fanning decimated the profit model of a $40 billion industry by releasing a program called Napster. It has forever changed the recording industry and the way music will be distributed in the future.*

> *FedEx no longer has the need to answer 700,000 phone calls today or to hire 20,000 additional people to handle the growth in package volumes. They also will not have to pay to print two billion forms or ship them to customers this year. Why? Because of FedEx software on the web, two thirds of all customer inquiries are answered by the customers themselves online! Customers are*

now entering shipping data, as well as printing their own bills, tracking packages, and checking billing information.

Polaroid, the company that came to define instant photography was blindsided by the rapid rise of digital photography. In October 2001 Polaroid filed for bankruptcy protection.

These pages could be filled with example after example of how companies, industries, and financial markets are being blindsided by change. Bill Gates in his book, *Business@the Speed of Thought* writes, "In three years every product we make will be obsolete. The only question is whether we'll make them obsolete or if someone else will." What's keeping you from being blindsided?

Let me give you one example of a company that recognized and responded to change. Apple Computer's CEO, Steve Jobs, took the fiercely competitive computer market, blended it with the music industry and released the iPod. Today, it is one of the most coveted personal gadgets in America. It's clever, it's cool, it oozes innovation, and it's created a new standard in how we purchase music.

Successful people realize that what happens may be out of your control, but what you do with what happens is completely up to you. It's your choice, just as it was the choice of the companies listed above. They could choose to dig in their heels and cling to the hope that things would never change, or they could recognize that learning and responding are the only sustainable competitive advantage they have.

How about you? Will you cling to a world that will no longer exist? Or, are you willing to learn and adopt The Currency of the Future?

Let me tell you what happened to me. Like most of us in our senior year, I went to see my high school counselor to seek guidance on that monumental question, "What am I going to do with my life?" In response, my counselor said, "You scored high in math and geometry. You should be an engineer." So, just like a lemming in line, I followed the conventional wisdom of the currency of the past and traipsed off to college to get a degree in Engineering. As an engineer, I made significantly

THE CURRENCY OF THE FUTURE

"In times of change, learners inherit the earth, while the learned find themselves beautifully equipped to deal with a world that no longer exists."

—Eric Hoffer

less money than I did working as a waiter and I was working twice the amount of hours! Not only that, I hated what I was doing! "How could this be?" I thought I was following the road to success. It wasn't long before I took my diploma off the wall and looked for something else.

I decided to start my own conventional business. The good news was that I made $100,000 my first full year in business! The bad news was that it cost me $180,000 to make it! On top of that, I had employees, overhead, office space, and inventory, and I was tied to my customers 24/7. So here I was, 27 years old, newly married, and $80,000 in debt! Talk about being ready for a change.

I was at a crossroads. I could take the familiar road and go back to being an Engineer or a waiter to spend the next 10 years of my life paying off the debt, or I could look for another way and take the unfamiliar road less traveled. I chose the latter, and that has made all the difference.

Reality Check

Be honest, haven't you had one of those moments? A moment when you ask yourself some of life's toughest questions? I remember driving home from my second job on a Saturday. I had recently started my career as an engineer and was working a second job for extra money. I was on the 15 freeway traveling south in the second lane when it happened. Both hands on the steering wheel, I thought to myself, "Is this it? Is this what life is going to be about for me? Driving back and forth to a job, doing my best to stay ahead, to keep afloat, and to pay the bills?"

Have you ever felt that way? Well, you're not alone. I read that over 86 percent of Americans say they dislike their jobs. Furthermore, a recent employment report by Harris Interactive stated that more than half of the workers surveyed said they feel "overtired and overwhelmed," and more than a quarter said they have trouble balancing their work and personal life.

Being tired makes everything that much more stressful, but it's like having a baby. You get used to it. It's kind of sad. The kids sometimes ask, "What's the deal with Dad? Does he still live here?" I've thought, "This is going to kill me." –Source: USA Today

"If you don't have hope for the future you have no power in the present." –John Maxwell

I have been practicing law for 14 years, and although I recently made partner at my firm, I want out. I've never liked the adversarial, antagonistic nature of what I do, and lately I'm so fed up with it I can barely drag myself to the office. But what else can I do? Are there opportunities in corporate America for legal refugees?
–Source: Fortune Magazine

For many American workers there is the concern of outsourcing. Employees forced to train their replacements say the practice is a stark illustration of how the hiring of foreign workers is plundering U.S. jobs. According to Forrester Research, in the next 15 years American employers will move about 3.3 million white-collar jobs and $136 billion in wages abroad.

When computer programmer Stephen Gentry learned last year that Boeing was laying him off, he wasn't too surprised, as many others in the company were experiencing the same fate. What really stunned him was his last assignment: managers had him train the worker from India who'd be taking his job. –Source: USA Today

Working a job they dislike, being overwhelmed, hopeless, and fearful of having the rug pulled out from under them–why? Why do so many people waste their precious lives for what fails to inspire them?

How about you? Are you just grinding it out day after day, or are you living on the edge and chasing a dream? Are you giving away the best hours of your life to a boss and a paycheck, or are you investing it in your future? One thing is certain: Security in the new economy will not be found in the traditional job.

"Stop going for the easy buck, and start producing something with your life. Create, instead of living off the buying and selling of others."
–Carl Fox in the movie Wall Street

WAKE UP AMERICA!

I'm often asked how I came up with the title of The Currency of the Future. It's simple, I got mad! This book is the result of total frustration! The more I saw the world change, the more I saw people ignore it. The more I saw the workplace change, the more I saw people digging-in their heels resisting it; and the more I saw technology increase, the more I saw people question it. My frustration comes from living in a time that is bursting with opportunity, yet so many people are sleeping right through it. I could have titled the book "WAKE UP AMERICA!"

It's like a marriage counselor trying to work with two stubborn people who are unwilling to take responsibility for their actions. Both of them are blaming each other and stuck in a rut, unwilling to change. Stubborn people don't grow and living in the past keeps you there.

The grocery workers are on strike, the phone company employees are picketing, and laid off workers are complaining. Is that The Currency of the Future? NO! Let's revisit the constitution for a moment, "life, liberty, and the PURSUIT of happiness." Some people ignore the word "pursuit" and think it's a guarantee, a hand-out, or something they have a right to just for being an American! If you're not making what you're worth, it's because you choose not to. My friend Bob says that society rewards you in proportion to your contribution to others. If you feel you're not receiving enough of a reward–that's a clue.

Are you being paid more or less than you think you are worth? If you answered less, what are you doing about it? Are you just complaining and demanding more? Or, maybe you're quietly waiting around for someone to notice you and how hard you've been working. Why don't *you* start noticing? Why don't *you* take control of your life and find a way to make what *you* think you're worth? After all, it's your life isn't it? I've heard it said that if you want to change some things in your life, then you have to change some things in your life! If you are willing to change, you can break through the paradigms that have limited you in the past and open up to a whole new world of opportunity. If you constantly avoid change or wait around for others to change, success will constantly avoid you.

12

"Individuals who will succeed and flourish will also be masters of change...." –Rosa McBeath-Canter, Harvard Business School

Now, notice I didn't say change is easy. It's hard work for most folks. Those who try to change are often faced with heavy resistance from all sides. The world wants you to remain average. But if you're reading this book, my guess is that you've already opened your mind to the prospect of change in your life. My guess is that you know in your heart that you are meant to experience more, more of what is important to you. Maybe...

More Money
More Freedom
More Fulfillment
More Travel
More Choices
More Time
More Influence

That's great! Discontentment is the catalyst for change, and people with a compelling reason to change, will.

Change is also uncomfortable isn't it? I think we'd all agree that no one really likes change. Okay, maybe there are a select few who thrive on it, and for those of you that do–go home and switch sides of the bed with your spouse before going to sleep tonight. On the other hand, are there instances where we do like change? How about your clothes? Do you wear the same thing every day? And do you eat the same meal every day? No. Then is it change that makes us uncomfortable, or is it our lack of control over change? Isn't it really the changes that we can't control, like layoffs and rapid technology we don't understand that makes us so uneasy? Well, the good news is that learning and applying The Currency of the Future will equip you to manage and control how change affects you. It's just what you need to launch you forward.

Recently, my wife and I visited the Hotel Del Coronado where I was employed as a waiter during my college years. The "Del," as they affectionately call it in San Diego, has been a landmark resort for over

13

110 years. It had been almost seven years since I left, yet I was overcome by a sense of déjà vu as I walked into the lobby one summer afternoon. I had worked as a waiter in the beautiful "Crown Room" and five nights a week I would put on a tuxedo to serve elegant food to hotel guests and visitors. This time, I had my shorts and Tommy Bahama Hawaiian shirt on as we walked around and admired the grand resort once again.

I didn't expect to see any of my past co-workers since it had been so long, but I couldn't resist the urge to peek into the Crown Room just once before leaving. To my surprise, almost the entire staff that I used to work with was still there! After a few handshakes and hellos, I saw Frank. Frank and I had worked together for many years and I can still remember how he complained about everything. "I hate this job." "Why don't they change this menu?" "Why do I always get the crummy shifts?" On and on he would go. I suppose that's why I was most surprised to see him still there.

I thought if anyone would have left and moved on it surely would have been Frank. He seemed so miserable, yet he hadn't changed a bit. Not two minutes into our conversation and he was already harping about something else, complaining and criticizing this and that. When he asked me what I was up to, I told him about the i-commerce business I had started. "Oh, nobody makes money in those things," he clamored. I just smiled to myself and as I turned to leave, I heard him say, "Don't get your hopes up!" I couldn't help but wonder, "Why is it that people can have so much MORE, but choose to settle for LESS?"

Some people never change. As Kim and I drove back home that day, I thought about the kind of life I might be living if I'd stayed at what my friends had called "The perfect job." Would I be driving my precious wife home in a luxury car to her dream home? Would we be spending our days together playing with our children? Would I be as passionate and excited about life? Would I be fulfilled? Not a chance. I'm glad I got my hopes up! If I had resisted change and listened to people like Frank, I would be driving home in the same old car to a rented apartment and both Kim and I would be heading off to a job the next day. We were thankful for the choices we made and the lifestyle it provided for our family. When we got home, we smiled and asked each other the same question we ask every day: "What do you feel like doing today?"

How about you? How would you spend your day if you were free? No deadlines looming, no boss to answer to, no financial pressure. What would you do today?

"Two roads diverged in a wood, and I took the one less traveled by, and that has made all the difference." –Robert Frost

THE
CURRENCY OF THE
FUTURE

> "In the 21st century, one of the most powerful forms of genius will be entrepreneurial genius...."
> –Dan Sullivan

Chapter II

IQ vs. "THE BIG THREE"

The Currency Of The Future confronts conventional wisdom about a career path and chucks it out the window! Your career, earning ability, and overall success in life have little to do with test scores, IQ, or in my case the "best guess" of my high school counselor.

In his book, *How the Best Get Better*, Dan Sullivan states, "There are different forms of genius: When most people hear the word genius they think of IQ–which measures genius in logical reasoning. However, there are many other forms of genius that are not measured by IQ: spatial, musical, kinesthetic, interpersonal, improvisational, and others. In the 21st century, one of the most powerful forms of genius will be entrepreneurial genius...."

Think about it: If intellectual intelligence (IQ) was the determining factor in our earning ability, wouldn't it stand to reason that college professors and rocket scientists would be the super rich? In fact, it's just the opposite. I've found that the A students often work for the C students. And the kid in my math class who was smarter than everyone else–he's working as a mail carrier now!

So why is it that people with ordinary talents often outperform those with greater physical and intellectual endowments? Do you remember Aesop's fable about the tortoise and the hare? The hare could run much faster than the tortoise, yet the tortoise won the race because he kept going and gave it everything he had. Sometimes people with ordinary talents become inspired and will work harder and longer than those with extraordinary talents. The tortoise just kept plodding toward the goal while the hare dallied along the way. The moral of the story? The race is not always won by the swift, nor do achievement and success always accrue to those with the nimblest wits and the highest IQs. In other words, what matters is a different way of being smart.

When I was a kid, I was pretty average just like the tortoise. No one would have called me a child-prodigy or specially gifted, and the only reason I scored well in school was that, like the turtle, I plodded along always making time to study. When I got to college, I knew I had to study more than my friends because I didn't have a high IQ. And because I didn't have a "mom and pop" scholarship, I had to work night shifts in restaurants to fund most of my college education. I can recall any number of times when my friends were at parties while I was plodding along learning life skills out in the real world. I never was a big shot; I was just a little shot that kept on shootin'.

I've seen so many "little shots" explode beyond the limitations of their conditions, yet the ones with all the looks or all the brains are often stymied in mediocrity. What people *can* do is astounding, but what they *will* do is often disappointing. It's like my friend Don–he had it all. He was a 4.0 in high school with a scholarship to a prestigious University. Talk about potential, this guy could write his ticket anywhere! Good looks, well spoken, and lots of charm, yet today he's unhappy in his career, recently ended his second marriage, and still can't find his niche in life.

Compare that to my friend Pedro who had all the odds stacked against him. He was born in Mexico and knew only poverty until his parents brought him to America. Like a kid in a candy store, he saw opportunity everywhere he looked. He started out working in restaurants washing dishes and diligently saved his money until he could afford to buy his first car. With what little he had, he began buying and selling cars to his friends and neighbors making a small profit on each sale. He then expanded his business by buying a car lot. Today, Pedro is financially independent and is experiencing phenomenal success with his thriving automobile dealership. He was just a little shot that kept on shootin'.

So, if brains aren't the key to success, then what is? I call them "The BIG 3." Emotional Intelligence (EQ), Financial Intelligence (FQ), and Relational Intelligence (RQ). Without question, your mastery of The BIG 3 will either make, or break your ability to create income in the future. The bad news is that they don't teach us about The BIG 3 in school. You'll have to earn these abilities at the University of Hard Knocks–that's right, real life experience along with a keen ear to the wisdom of the ages. Skills, not theories, will make you wealthy. The good news is that, unlike IQ, they can be learned by anyone.

Schooling vs. Education

Personally, I'm not impressed with how much college education someone has. Many of my wealthy friends never even finished school. In fact, they're in good company; Bill Gates, Michael Dell, Steve Jobs, and Ted Turner were also dropouts. Earlier entrepreneurs such as Thomas Edison and Henry Ford never finished school either.

Yet every year, thousands of young Americans are graduating this country's fine institutions with a degree in their hand and a misconception that they've got their ticket to a successful career. Most of them are completely unaware of how ill equipped they really are to face the challenges ahead. And those who are already established in their careers believe the solution to their challenges is more schooling. Wake up! The industrial age is long gone. Today's society has advanced and the world's workforce is realizing more and more that what really matters is a person's emotional, financial, and relational intelligence.

Now, don't get me wrong. I'm not against a college education. I just think that a University diploma is highly over-rated. Are you looking to develop skills in wealth thinking or poverty management? Here's what I found: My University education taught me working class values and how to become a marketable *employee*. In contrast, my rich friends saw the real world as a more exciting place to get their education and experience. And in reality, the adventurous side of me liked the element of risk involved in the real world better than sitting in a predictable classroom all day anyway.

Scientists will tell you that your IQ is set at birth and no matter how much you study, it may only increase a few points. Don't ever let things like that discourage you from believing that you can expand your thinking. The BIG 3, not IQ, will be the new yardstick of measure in tomorrow's marketplace. You can start increasing your value right now by reading through this chapter and applying the skills and principles discussed in it today. You're off on your first undertaking to developing your Currency Of The Future!

Emotional Intelligence (EQ)

Ah... the emotions. The charge of victory, the passion of love, the excitement of a new adventure! Aren't they what make life so spectacular? But what about when life starts to heat up? Do you breakdown and lose control or do you maintain your "cool"? EQ is our ability to take a few shots on the chin and keep moving forward. How well we govern our behavior is one of the chief indicators of our success. No matter what work you currently do, your emotional intelligence is crucial to your marketability as an employee or a business owner.

In the past, experts viewed thinking and feeling as polar opposites–logic on one side and passion on the other. Emotions were labeled as unpredictable, haphazard, and immature. Today, modern research has discredited this view and found that our ability to monitor our feelings and emotions, to discriminate among them, and to use this information to guide our thinking and action is critical to our overall intelligence system. In his book, *Emotional Intelligence*, Daniel Goleman argues that our emotions play a much greater role in thought, decision making, and individual success than is commonly acknowledged. He defines "emotional intelligence," a trait that is not measured by IQ tests, as a set of skills including: control of one's impulses, self-motivation, empathy, and social competence. Goleman downplays the significance of IQ and asserts that our view of human intelligence is far too narrow, ignoring a crucial range of abilities which are of greater consequence to how well we do in life.

Growing up in the home of a football coach, I would often overhear the phone conversations my father had with other coaches and talent scouts. They would frequently discuss the essential qualities of an athlete, and

THE
CURRENCY OF THE
FUTURE

"I have never let my schooling interfere with my education."
–Mark Twain

one of those qualities was emotional toughness. They wanted to know if a man would stay tough mentally and perform despite the challenges on and off the field, and whether or not he could take coaching and direction professionally. I learned from my father early on that physical strength, speed, and agility often took a backseat to someone's EQ.

How's your EQ? Have you ever found yourself in a conversation where someone sharply criticized you or challenged your viewpoint? What happened to your emotions? Did they go up? What happened to your intelligence? I'll bet that it went down. Are you *reacting* or *responding* in those moments when you find yourself "put on the spot" and flustered? Those are the moments when your EQ is tested.

My four-year-old, Brady, learned this lesson recently when my wife and I took our three kids to get their passports for a family trip to Fiji and Australia. Summer came early this year with a 105 degree blast of heat in May and we all felt it when we stepped out of our air-conditioned SUV. As we made our way across the parking lot, Brady started complaining about the heat. Without missing a beat, my five-year-old princess, Bailey, turned to Brady and said, "Stop complaining. Life's not fair!" That was one of the proudest moments I've had as a parent! I smiled to myself and thought, "Yes! My kids are learning emotional toughness."

Over the years, I've had the privilege of being a personal coach to a number of business owners and partners in my industry. While sitting down one-to-one strategizing with them and doing my best to assist them in their careers, I frequently found myself frustrated with how to give them advice. I knew they were implementing all of the required tasks and accomplishing the activity needed to succeed, but for some reason the results weren't there. Where was the breakdown? What was the problem? They were making the calls, clocking the miles, and saying all the right things, but their averages were terrible. Most of them could have outperformed me any day of the week, yet they were floundering. What was it?

Here's what I found: They talked too much and listened too little; they mechanically executed the tasks, but lacked the magic of a simple smile; they had talent, but no passion. If they were questioned, they'd talk over

THE
CURRENCY OF THE
FUTURE

"Stop complaining. Life's not fair!"
–Bailey DeHaven

people or argue; if people were reluctant, they'd shove it down their throats a little harder; and if someone showed interest, they'd overdo it and talk them right out of it–all from a lack of emotional control. These failing or marginal performances were all marked by an inability to ignite the interest or passions of others. These people were all smart, but didn't have the "street smarts" of communication. They were not failing logically, but emotionally.

They were letting their emotions affect their interaction with others. Just like those funny mirrors you see at the circus that make you look tall, short, wide, or slim–your emotions can distort your view of reality and sabotage your ability to understand and connect with others. The qualities that mark people who excel in life are self-awareness, impulse control, persistence, zeal, self-motivation, empathy, and social deftness. People who master these qualities will begin to see their relationships flourish.

Take Things Professionally, Not Personally

So how about you? How would you rank your EQ? Do you throw in the towel when you're faced with adversity? Do you lose your cool, become defensive, angry, and blow off steam? Or, are you like the swan who maintains its gracefulness and serenely moves across the water even when its legs are swiftly paddling below the surface? I often refer to EQ as developing "thick skin." If rejection and ridicule rattle your cage, it's time to toughen up and develop your emotional intelligence. Learn to take things professionally, not personally. Remember that people don't do things to you, they do things for themselves.

"Once you embrace unpleasant news, not as a negative but as evidence of a need for change, you aren't defeated by it. You're learning from it." –Bill Gates

Did you know that it's your choice to perceive things any way you choose? You are in the driver's seat of your mind–or at least you should be! Why not decide to take rejection as a source of valuable feedback and improvement instead of as a personal attack on you? Why not use adversity as your reason, instead of your excuse? Is it possible to take some of that steam you're blowing and use it in a more creative way to produce positive results?

Jay Leno, the talk show host of *The Tonight Show* did just that. When he replaced Johnny Carson on the show, he took a lot of heat from critics. He was compared unfavorably to Carson, and many people expected that his career would be short-lived. Surprisingly, Leno maintained a high EQ. He even kept a stack of unpleasant reviews on his desk for motivation. One review read "Too many soft questions." Another said, "He's being too nice." These unkind words never bothered Leno. Why? Because they were written in 1962 and were directed at Jack Paar's replacement–"An awkward nobody named Johnny Carson."

Leno had an above average EQ and it has served him well. The average EQ, on the other hand, is affected by every change in their environment. Just like a thermometer, they go up when it heats up and they cool down when everything around them is calm. The key is for you to be in control–be the thermostat and set your own optimum temperature.

Rather than identifying with everyone around you, have confidence in who you are. Instead of trying to accommodate and please everyone else, make a decision to be comfortable in your own skin. So often people suppress their thoughts, ideas, unique qualities, and authenticity out of fear. They are afraid that they will lose acceptance if they are different or if they disagree with what someone else thinks. True as that may be, you will never discover your true potential or your greatest qualities by appeasing others. Be at ease whether you are talking to a child or a successful business person, whether rich or poor, friend or foe. When opportunity arises, be true to your self, your beliefs, your passions, and allow yourself the chance to genuinely engage in life by confidently being you.

"Dignity and Respect has to do with what you are ready, willing, and able to accept within yourself and in accepting to be able to give others. It is your personal power to make a difference by being true to the best within you and letting that truth shine through your words and actions." –Gail Pursell Elliott

Financial Intelligence (FQ)

FQ, like EQ and RQ, is a different way of being smart. In the new economy, financial planning doesn't start with financial projections; it begins with the end in mind. What is your ultimate objective? Ben Stein said, "The indispensable first step to getting the things you want out of life is this: Decide what you want." Take the time to figure out where you want to go before you decide how you're going to get there–it's simple common sense, but one that so few actually practice. In developing your Currency of the Future, a dream is the one thing that you must have in the bank. How's your account?

I know what you're thinking. "Don't give me this dreamy weamy stuff Brad. Take off the rose colored glasses and get real!" I agree, let's get real. Look around over the next week to spot everyone you can over 65 years of age. Every time you see them ask yourself this question, "Do I want to be living the way they are when I am 65?" You'll find what statistics have proven for decades: 95 percent of Americans retire at a standard of living much LESS than what they had when they were working. In plain English, here are the cold hard facts: People are not making it financially!

How can this be? We live in the land of opportunity in an age where financial information is at our fingertips! What's wrong? For starters, let's look at the home where learning begins. What is being taught in the average American home about financial independence, business ownership, and the pursuit of your dream? How about in our public school system, what are they teaching about financial intelligence and working smart? The obvious answer is *nothing*.

I started understanding how deluded I had been when I asked one of my mentors about a financial issue. After he gave me his advice I said, "That's not normal, who does that?" He smiled and made this point: "Brad, if you do what everyone else is doing, you're doing something wrong because everyone isn't making it."

Those comments really hit home and as I ventured out to develop my business, people would tell me things like, "Brad, what are you doing that for?" "That's not normal." "If you're so right then why isn't everyone else doing it?" I was actually thankful for some of those reactions because I began to understand the simple lesson, *Think Different*. If everyone else (the 95%) doesn't "GET-IT," there's a good chance you're on the right track! Anatole France said, "If a million people say a foolish thing, it is still a foolish thing." In other words, a majority, in and of itself, doesn't necessarily make something true.

Where is Your Thinking?

We've been conditioned throughout life to become employees. We're told that to become successful, we must go to school, get an "education," look for a safe, secure job with benefits that will put a roof over our heads, food on the table, and a nice car in the driveway. Robert Kiyosaki, best-selling author of *Rich Dad, Poor Dad* says that if you believe that, you still believe in Santa Claus and the Easter Bunny.

Kiyosaki is a wealthy entrepreneur and the only author to claim the top three spots on the *New York Times* best-seller list at the same time. He has become famous for explaining financial literacy in easy-to-understand terms. Take a look at the following diagram of the "CASHFLOW Quadrant."

Source: Rich Dad's CASHFLOW Quadrant™
ESBI symbol is a trademark of CASHFLOW Technologies, Inc.
All Rights Reserved

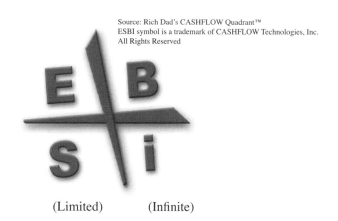

(Limited)   (Infinite)

In his book, *Cashflow Quadrant*, Kiyosaki outlines four ways to create income. He explains that about 95 percent of the population finds themselves generating income from the left side of the quadrant as an **Employee** or **Self-employed**, while only 5 percent generate income through the right two quadrants titled **Business Owner** and **Investor**. On the left side of the quadrant, you exchange your time and expertise for money. On the right side of the quadrant, systems make your money work for you.

If you are an **Employee**, you *work for a system* exchanging your time for money. What happens when you stop working? You stop making money. And who has the leverage, you or the company you work for? The company. They hire you at wholesale and then sell your labor at retail. Who determines your wholesale price–how much you're worth? The company or your boss does. The real question is: Who should decide what you are worth? YOU SHOULD! My mentor put it this way, "Every business has enough room for one dream. If it's not your business, it's not your dream."

If you are **Self-employed** (Small business), *you are the system*. The problem with the **S** quadrant is that if you're not exchanging your expertise, your system is not making your money work for you. You may, theoretically, have more control compared to an **Employee**, but you're still trading your time for money. And what about taking time off as a **Small** business owner? Forget it! No one is paying you for sick days or two weeks vacation in the **S** quadrant. You end up running yourself into the ground, working all the time until one day, you do the math and figure out that you're not going to get ahead doing what you are doing. After seeing the CASHFLOW Quadrant for the first time, a friend of mine who owns a law firm in Chicago said, "I have made a total **S** of myself!"

Bottom line, no matter how hard you work as an **Employee** or a **Self-employed** small business owner, your income and freedom are constrained. Time is a limited commodity and the people on the right side of the quadrant understand that.

So, what is it that people on the right side of the quadrant do differently? They work smarter by devoting their resources up-front to building a *system that works for them* indefinitely. While only 5 percent of people are **B**s and **I**s, they make 95 percent of the money in this country. I believe that success leaves clues and this one is crystal clear. The right side of the quadrant earns 95 percent of the money!

Business owners leverage systems that do the hard work for them–not the other way around. Bill Gates didn't get rich selling software; Bill Gates got rich building a system. There is a vast difference between somebody who has been conditioned to think like an **E**mployee versus somebody who has been conditioned to think like a **B**usiness owner. They think differently. For most people, the hardest part of transitioning to the right side of the quadrant is in shifting from **E**mployee mentality to **B**usiness owner mentality.

Just as a doctor will learn different skills than an accountant, to become a **B**usiness owner you must learn different skills and attitudes than an employee. This is the essence of The Currency of the Future and what this book is all about: To help you understand how to think like a **B**usiness owner. It is a personal decision. You can either work all your life to be poor, or you can change your thinking and work to be rich. The choice is yours.

The table on the following page outlines the difference in thinking between the left and right sides of the CASHFLOW Quadrant. Where does your thinking and activity line up?

When I first looked at the Quadrant, I remember wondering if I was an **S** or a **B**. I asked my mentor about it and he helped me clarify things by suggesting that I join him on a two-week vacation. My mind immediately started reeling at just the thought of taking two weeks off. "I can't leave my business for that long! My clients need me. I'll lose income. Who's going to pay the bills?" *"Exactly."* He said, "Your earning power is 100 percent on the left side. To move to the right side you need to have a system that continues to create income without your presence. To become financially independent, you need to make yourself insignificant."

LEFT QUADRANT THINKING	RIGHT QUADRANT THINKING
Immediate payoff	The right payoff
Instant gratification	Delayed gratification
Guaranteed methods	Results producing, calculated risks
Tension relieving activities	Goal achieving activities
Spend money on trivial things	Spend money on income producing investments
Fun, easy, enjoyable	Hard, necessary, important
Self gratification	Self discipline
Sell your time	Leverage your time
Work for a system	Have a system work for you

Source: Rich Dad's CASHFLOW Quadrant™
ESBI symbol is a trademark of CASHFLOW
Technologies, Inc. All Rights Reserved

THE CURRENCY OF THE FUTURE

"I would rather have 1 percent of 100 men's efforts than 100 percent of my own."
–J. Paul Getty

Relational Intelligence (RQ)

Excluding the rare individual that isolates themselves in a dark hole, wouldn't you agree that we all continually have to connect with others in one way or another? Relational intelligence is our capacity to connect with other people in a skillful, warm, and authentic way. As relational beings we are made to enjoy friendship and community with others, and the person with an above average RQ puts a high value on cultivating and understanding those relationships. More than anything else, your RQ will determine your overall happiness and fulfillment in life.

How's your RQ? Do you take notice of those around you? Do you smile as you greet your employees or the people you run into at the grocery store or café? Do the people you talk to feel heard, understood, respected, and valued? I'll always remember the lesson Mr. Gonzalez taught me in my first Engineering course. After studying material strengths of concrete and steel for weeks, he gave us our first exam. As I breezed through the questions, I knew I'd score well on the exam; after all, I was a conscientious student. I knew I had it made–until I read the last question:

"What is the first name of the janitor who cleans our building?"

What is this a joke? I'd seen the janitor several times and could picture him in my mind. He was short, dark-haired, and in his fifties. But how, and more importantly, *why* would I know his name?

I handed in my paper leaving the last question blank. And just before class ended, one of the students asked what we were all wondering: "Does the last question count toward our grade?" "Absolutely!" The professor expained, "In your careers you will meet many people; all are significant. They deserve your attention and care, even if all you do is smile and say 'hello.'"

I've never forgotten that lesson. I also learned his name was Larry.

This wise professor understood that relationship skills would play a vital role in the success of his students as they progressed in life.

THE CURRENCY OF THE FUTURE

"People who invest themselves in relational greatness–those who have deep friendships with people they laugh and cry with, learn together with, achieve and fail with, dance and grow with, and live and die with– these are people who lead magnificent lives."

–John Ortberg

So, how do we give our relationships the attention and care they deserve? Start by consciously making relationships a priority in your life. To become strong in the RQ department, we have to take relational initiatives with others instead of waiting around for them to reach out to us. This will be tough! I have often found myself thinking, "If they really want to talk, they can call *me*," or "If this business is important to them, they will seek *me* out," and "If my product has value to them, they will call *me*." To successfully connect with others, you will have to dump these emotions and take the initiative.

Identify the key relationships in your life and decide to better connect with those people who are important to you. Take a moment to call them and see how they are doing–and make that the only reason for your call. Send them a card just to let them know you are thinking of them. You'll be amazed at what a difference these small and seemingly insignificant connections will make.

The strength of your relationships will increase over time as you continually connect with others and reaffirm to them that you care. You can't microwave a business relationship, a friendship, a marriage, or raising kids. Building trust, listening, problem solving, and loving others all require time and cannot be rushed.

Another way to increase your RQ is by simply learning to shift your focus from yourself onto others. Instead of trying to get what you want, find out what they want. Instead of thinking about what you can get, think about how you can help others to achieve what they want. Understand that people care about themselves more than they care about helping you. So, if you want someone's interest, be interested in them.

Think about it: Who do you prefer to do business with–someone who is genuine and comfortable to talk to that is interested in your needs, or the person who puts on an act, cuts you off, and gives you their spiel? The answer is obvious.

"You can have everything in life you want if you will only help enough other people get what they want." –Zig Ziglar

As we add value to the lives of others, we in turn develop one of our greatest assets: a network of established relationships. And the greater your network, the greater the support, ideas, information, advice, referrals, resources, and leverage you possess. Not all relationships will be reciprocal. Know that you will give more than you receive. But what comes around goes around and as you continue to invest in the lives of others, you will increase your network and your ability to succeed.

Managing relationships will likely prove to be one of the most challenging aspects of your journey. The fact is, relationships are hard to assemble because people are hard to assemble. It's like herding cats; it's never easy. Everyone has quirks, blind spots, and is weird in some areas. So, if you're going to connect with people, you are going to connect with quirky, broken, weird people. Let's face it, those are the only kind of people there are!

As difficult and demanding as relationships may be, investing in them is one of the greatest and most rewarding things you will ever do. If your journey is anything like my own, your most significant sense of accomplishment will come from knowing that you have made a difference in the lives of others.

Roast Marshmallows

There was a nine-year study conducted on relationships engineered by a Harvard social scientist. The research took place in Alameda County, California and studied over 7,000 people. The results were astounding! They found that the most isolated people were three times more likely to die an early death than the most relationally connected people. Not only that, the study revealed that people who had bad health habits like smoking, poor eating patterns, obesity, and alcohol, who maintained strong relational connections lived significantly longer than those who had great health habits but were isolated.

In other words, it's better to roast marshmallows with friends than to eat spinach salad alone!

The human experience was meant for relational connectedness. We're all designed to love and be loved, to know and be known, to serve and be served, to celebrate and be celebrated. Anything else you accomplish, no matter how much stuff you pile up, or how high you climb on the ladder of success—you will miss the fullness of life without it.

Ask anyone on their "deathbed" what really matters most. I guarantee you that the conversation won't be about trophies, career positions, or possessions. That person with the most revealing perspective will talk to you about who they loved and who loved them.

Perhaps above all, relationally intelligent people understand the brevity of life. They live in awareness that one day life will end. Maybe it'll be cancer or a heart that just stops beating. Maybe it'll be a car that misses a stop sign or simply a human body that has lived its course. But one thing is for sure, if you get your RQ right, whatever you mess up, no matter how miserable your finances, or how horribly you fail in business—you will have won. On the other hand, if you never develop your RQ, whatever title came after your name, or how big your office or home—you will have lost.

Still don't believe me? Just look at the brave soldiers on D-day during World War II. What were they clutching in their fists as they lay there dying on that beach in Normandy? What was it that they needed to see just one last time in those final moments? Soldier after soldier was found gripping a picture of their family or a letter that a loved one had sent them.

Regardless of where you are in your relationships today, or what has happened to your relationships in the past, don't let it end without genuinely connecting with others.

I love the following story because it reminds me of the relational giving of children.

Many years ago, when I worked as a volunteer at a hospital, I got to know a little girl named Janessa who was suffering from a rare and serious disease. Her only chance of recovery appeared to be a blood transfusion from her five-year-old brother, who had miraculously survived the same disease and had developed the

36

antibodies needed to combat the illness. The doctor explained the situation to her little brother, and asked the little boy if he would be willing to give his blood to his sister.

I saw him hesitate for only a moment before taking a deep breath and saying, "Yes I'll do it if it will save her." As the transfusion progressed, he lay in bed next to his sister and smiled, as we all did, seeing the color returning to her cheeks. Then his face grew pale and his smile faded.

He looked up at the doctor and asked with a trembling voice, "Will I start to die right away?"

Being young, the little boy had misunderstood the doctor; he thought he was going to have to give his sister all of his blood in order to save her.

"People don't care how much you know until they know how much you care." –John Maxwell

Your Seven Keys
to Developing The Currency of the Future

Chapter III
Find Your Reason

It was a warm summer afternoon over 10 years ago. I remember it as if it was yesterday because that was the day I would meet my millionaire mentor. And that was the day the direction of my life changed forever. After surfing that morning, I made it home early to meet with a guy to discuss a business project he was working on. I'd never met him before, but he was a good friend of my mother's from Ohio and we had spoken on the phone a few weeks earlier. We met at a Chili's restaurant where he briefly discussed a business idea and sketched out a few illustrations on the back of a napkin. What has transpired from that meeting is absolutely mind-blowing to me. I learned more about business, life, and success from a napkin in a Chili's restaurant than I did in six years of college and two degrees! Today, that chicken scratch has turned into a multi-million dollar business for my family.

What's most impressive to me isn't the size of our business; countless others have accomplished that. Rather, the person that I have become. How can someone like me, who was so shy, self-centered, and cynical, grow into a person that can comfortably speak to thousands of people about developing their currency of the future? How is that possible? What my mentor understood and explained to me that day was that *reasons come first, answers come second*. Read that again, because it is the most significant component to developing your Currency of the

Future. I never could have journeyed from where I was to where I am today without a burning desire and a strong reason to drive me.

At first, my mentor's language perplexed me. It didn't make any sense! His line of questioning puzzled me because I was fresh out of college and the interviewing process. "Why does he care about my reasons, my goals, and life passions? What does that have to do with my value in the marketplace? And why isn't he impressed with my GPA and senior project? I thought we were going to talk about a business project. Why would any valid business idea sit backseat to someone's dreams or passions? Don't you have to understand the business model, its marketing plan, its profit potential, the company vision, its details... details... details... before anything else? Aren't these the issues that are important when evaluating any business?"

Reasons come first, answers come second. It made total sense to him. My mentor wanted to know what made me tick. He explained, "Why would I show you something different if you don't want anything different?" Think about it: Why would he invest time in a business partner who had no desire for more? Why would he invest money in developing his company across the country unless he had a teachable, motivated partner to run it? Anyone can learn to operate a business, yet a man or a woman with a burning desire pounding within their heart is a much more rare and valuable commodity. Emerson summarized it this way, "What lies behind us and what lies before us are tiny matters compared to what lies within us."

See, most people get it wrong–they get it backwards. The currency of the past suggests that you work hard in a good job, pay your bills, and then take whatever is left over and use that towards your family's lifestyle. Use your leftover time to spend with your spouse and children, your left over money to determine the size and location of your home, your vacations, your health care, and on and on. Isn't your family sick of getting leftovers? This thought process, my friend, is the single biggest mistake I see people make in their life choices. They want logic before passion; they want answers before reasons. You see in life, everything begins with the heart.

THE
CURRENCY OF THE
FUTURE

"The two most important days in someone's life
are the day that they are born and the day
they discover why."

–John Maxwell

Through mentorship and countless hours of reading, listening, and associating with positive, successful people, I've been able to step into the life that was my reason years ago. The picture that I had embedded in my mind is what I began to shape my life around. Part of that picture was to be a husband and father who could experience one of life's most precious rewards of participating in his children's growing years. *Dreams do come true.* Our three children have never seen mom or dad walk out the door to go and work a job for someone else. That is priceless! I am so grateful that someone thought enough of me to give me a chance–the chance to earn what I was worth and pursue The Currency of the Future to live my best life.

What's your reason? Does it grip you and move you emotionally when you think about it? Does it keep you up at night and distract you during the day? What inspires you? Do you have something worth fighting for or someone worth winning for? What is your life going to be all about? What is your purpose and what do you want others to say about you when you are gone?

Take a moment and crystallize your reason by imagining your life of success. What does it look like? Indulge yourself in a daydream for the first time in ages. Let your mind wander beyond the "realities"– remember it's a daydream! Are there tears of joy on a loved one's face? How do you feel? Relieved? Excited? Alive again? Or maybe you're relaxed watching the sky turn tangerine orange as the sun sets on tropical waters, or you're casting a fishing line on a perfectly still mountain lake as dawn breaks–go ahead and picture it. Now use the power of that image to recommit yourself to your potential.

"A man's mind, stretched by a new idea, can never go back to its original dimension." -Oliver Wendell Holmes

The Achievement Cycle

While no one knows precisely how their lives will turn out, we can pre-program ourselves to become the kind of person we want to become and to live the life we want to live. Our thoughts determine our actions, which in turn determine our lives. Having this "bigger picture" can pull us through some of the short-term challenges and keep things in perspective. It is a significant source in driving you to achieve your dreams.

This process reminds me of the sculptor who was finishing a monument of a famous man on his horse in the town square. As he was working away, hammer and chisel in hand, an admiring onlooker asked him, "What a marvelous talent you have. How did you do it?" The sculptor replied, "I just chisel off everything that doesn't look like the man on his horse."

By envisioning yourself living a successful life, you become the master sculptor of your future.

Try this great exercise to help open your mind to what's important to you. I challenge you to make a list of 100 things you want to have, do, or become. Writing down the things that are important to you is acknowledging to your conscious and subconscious mind that where you are is not where you want to be.

Let me give you an example of some of the things on my list of 100:

1. To have more influence on my kids than anyone else.
2. To be remembered as a "great encourager."
3. To help 100 families become financially independent.
4. To give 1 million dollars in one year to charities.
5. To build a surfing wave pool on my property.
6. To learn how to speak Spanish.
7. To have 1,000 palm trees surrounding my home.
8. To paint a 15' x 15' mural on the wall above our Jacuzzi bath tub.
9. To become the only man that my wife would want to have an affair with.
10. To be a hero to my three children.

What I learned from my mentor and from most of the successful entrepreneurs in the world is that they organize their thinking differently. Take a look at the illustration below called "The Achievement Cycle."

Everything begins with a reason–your DREAM. Next are the road markers on the way to your dream called GOALS. The strategy to accomplish your goals is your PLAN. The final part is simply the EFFORT that is required to turn the cycle. That's the Achievement Cycle. It's the right *way* to think, and it's the right *order* to think.

As you look at this diagram, can you see where you may have been off track in your thinking before? Have you ever decided not to do something worthwhile because you focused on the EFFORT first? Are you guilty of ever becoming discouraged about a great idea after over analyzing the PLAN? Or maybe, you focused on the GOAL first, only to realize after achieving it that you'd steered your life in the wrong direction. These are all common mistakes that are made when we don't follow the Achievement Cycle.

Let's look at a few examples of how the Achievement Cycle works:

DREAM: Let's say your dream is to pursue your passion in music. You want to be able to have enough passive income to live out the rest of your life writing and composing music. You would have a custom built log cabin in the mountains with a state of the art recording studio.

GOAL: You're pretty ambitious, so you set a goal to achieve your dream in 5 years.

PLAN: You're currently working at a music equipment store and the owner has offered to promote you to "General Manager." You also give private guitar lessons on weekends for extra money.

EFFORT: You're working two jobs and willing to do whatever it takes!

What's wrong with this picture? Your PLAN doesn't match your GOAL or DREAM! No matter how well you do in your jobs, it will never net out the financial results that your dream requires. What's the solution? Find a better PLAN! Never downsize your DREAM to match your PLAN–that brings you right back to the *wrong* kind of thinking, or what I call "The Perpetual Cycle." The Perpetual Cycle is just like a hamster wheel. No matter how hard you run, you never actually get anywhere because you're running on the wrong track.

Here's another example:

DREAM: You and your spouse dream of becoming financially free so you can spend the rest of your lives enjoying your success and traveling the world together.

GOAL: Replace both of your incomes in 8 years by developing passive income in your new web-based business venture.

PLAN: To consistently work evenings and weekends together until your business is solidified and capable of running itself.

EFFORT: You had a great start getting your business off the ground with the initial excitement you both had. But lately, you are disagreeing on the particulars of exactly who is responsible for what and how things should be done. You and your spouse are growing increasingly bitter and resentful about your conflicting views on the right way to advertise your business. You now spend most of your time coming up with creative new ways to aggravate your spouse.

The problem here is obvious. You're both missing the big picture. Sometimes you have to let go of the little things in order to achieve the big things that really matter. You may be able to accomplish some things individually, but your dream requires accomplishing great things together.

Let's look at one final example:

DREAM: As a husband and father, your dream is to have enough money and freedom to spend ample time with your children while enjoying a fabulous lifestyle together as a family.

GOAL: Your goal is to become one of the top executives with your company in 5 years.

PLAN: You plan on delegating more work to others and focusing your attention on increasing bottom line results.

EFFORT: Your diligent efforts are being noticed by executives and your overtime hours and extra travel are earning you a solid reputation with the company. Unfortunately, you've missed most of your kids' activities over the last two years and the strain on your marriage is really starting to take its toll.

What's wrong? You've sold your soul to a career and are so focused on your GOAL that you've lost sight of your DREAM. Always keep your GOALS within the proper perspective of your DREAM.

Mr. Success

This example reminds me of the following story from Og Mandino's book *The Choice*:

It was the story of Mark Christopher, the youngest vice-president of his company, who was responsible for eighty-four branch offices throughout New England and the sales production of more than seven hundred salespeople. While providing a great lifestyle for his family, he spent his time traveling, working long hours, and teaching a class at a University. He had been nicknamed "Mr. Success." Mark was up early that Father's Day morning catching a short breakfast with his two young boys before running out for a round of golf with some of his associates.

As I watched and listened to the two of them, a strange feeling came over me. Glenn, my twelve-year-old, seemed to be aging before my eyes. Or maybe it was just the first time I had taken a good look at him since I couldn't remember when. He was handsome and, luckily for him, was getting to look more and more like his mother. Gosh had he grown up. There was even a hint of fuzz above his upper lip; his hands seemed immense, and his voice had a break in it. Between my long hours at the office and university plus my weekends on the golf course, I hadn't noticed his gradual transition from the infant I once bathed every night to the young man who now sat before me. The horrible thought suddenly hit me that he would be off to college in five years and more or less out of my life in ten.

I turned my attention to Todd who was struggling to read aloud from the back of his giant cereal box. He was already in the first grade. It was only yesterday, wasn't it, that I had paced the floor outside the delivery room until I heard his first cry? Where did those six years go? He glanced up from his cereal bowl, and all I could see were those big brown eyes, cloned directly from his mother. For the first time I noticed how red his hair had become. Todd returned my stare with a frown. "What's the matter, Dad, don't you like the cards?"

I assured him that they were great, the very best Father's Day cards I had ever seen. Then I heard the horn. The guys had arrived. I stood, gave them both another hug, and headed toward the garage.

They followed me. When I reached the driveway, Todd said, "Play a good game!", and Glenn shouted, "I hope you win!"

I waved and walked down the driveway toward the awaiting car. Bob leaped out of the driver's side to open the back gate in his station wagon for my golf clubs. I said "Good morning" and a few other words. Bob frowned, angrily shook his head, and got back in the car, slamming the door. He gunned the motor and roared off. I stood there in my Arnold Palmer shirt with pants to match hardly comprehending what I had done. Watching me from the garage, as puzzled as I was, stood my two pajama-clad boys.

Finally, Todd came running down the driveway and leaped into my arms. I buried my face in his small chest until he pushed my head back and asked, "Daddy, why are you crying?"

What could I say to him? How could I tell him that my tears were for all those hours and days and years I had spent on all the projects and sales meetings and golf courses that would still be there long after my two little men became big men and left me forever?

Mark Christopher went on to change some things in his life and pursue his dreams. *Will you*?

What we can learn from each of these examples is that you must hold tight to your dream first and foremost! Cultivate it, touch it, feel it, write it down, post pictures of it, become passionate about it, and believe that you can have, do, or become it. Most importantly, use the desire for your dream to fuel your creativity on how you will achieve it.

"Increase the size of your dream everyday and spend the rest of your life chasing after it." –unknown

In the movie *Pearl Harbor*, there is a scene where President Roosevelt meets with his top military advisors to determine the best strategy for a return attack on Japan. He is determined to hit the heart of Japan and asks his advisors for a plan. One by one, they all fold to the "reality" that it can not be done. "We don't have a place to launch our planes."

"Our ships can't get close enough." "Our Navy is now crippled and vulnerable..."

As President Roosevelt listens to his advisors' responses, his anger grows and fuels the intensity of his resolve. The final statement from one of his advisors, "Mr. President, with all respect, what you are asking can't be done..." is the last straw. With inhuman strength, the President extends his leg braces, struggles up to a standing position from the wheelchair that polio had dealt him, pushes it aside, and says, "Do not tell me it can't be done!"

Show me a person with dreams backed by passion, conviction, and resolve, and I'll show you a winner.

THE CURRENCY OF THE FUTURE

"I'm not looking for the best players.
I'm looking for the right players."

–Quote from the film *Miracle*

Chapter IV
Turn "Me" Into "We"

L ife and business are a team sport and cooperative teamwork is an integral part of any successful venture. While you may win a game or two on your own, it takes a team to win the championship. Teamwork is the joint action and cooperation of its members where each person sees the other person's success as a means for the attainment of their own. The Currency of the Future increases in value when we learn to leverage ourselves by linking up in empowering teams.

You can't whistle a symphony, nor can you create your life's masterpiece without the valuable instruments of a team. Thomas Edison, when asked why he had a team of twenty-one assistants replied, "If I could solve all the problems myself, I would." Like Edison, there will come a time in your journey when you realize that the possibilities are limited when you rely on your efforts alone. Whether it is a decorated war veteran, an Olympic medal winner, or a successful entrepreneur, you'll always discover the ultimate evidence of their success—the team. They beat the odds when "me" became "we."

The reasons to work as a team are endless. More people means more ideas, more perspective, more insight, more energy, more resources, the list goes on and on. And through its collaborative efforts, a team multiplies the value of its individual members producing significantly greater results than if they were to go at it alone.

The following is one my favorite stories on teamwork:

An out-of-towner accidentally drove his car into a deep ditch on the side of a country road. Luckily, a farmer happened by with his big old horse named Betsy and offered to help him pull his car out. The farmer backed Betsy up and hitched her to the car bumper. He yelled, "Pull, Nellie, pull!" Betsy didn't move. Then he yelled, "Come on Ranger. Pull!" Betsy still didn't move. "Now pull, Fred. Pull hard!" Betsy just stood there. Finally, the farmer said, "Okay, Betsy, pull!" Betsy pulled and the car came right out of the ditch. The man was very appreciative, but curious. He asked the farmer why he called his horse by the wrong name three times. The farmer replied, "Oh, Betsy is blind, and if she thought she was the only one pulling, she never would have tried."

We all pull harder when we're working as a team. I've heard that one large Clydesdale horse can pull a 2,000 pound wagon by itself. Two Clydesdales harnessed together, pulling in the same direction will pull 20,000 pounds! Working as a cooperative team, they accomplish ten times more than they would as one.

"Teamwork is the ability to work together toward a common vision. The ability to direct individual accomplishment toward organizational objectives. It is the fuel that allows common people to attain uncommon results." –Andrew Carnegie

Teamwork = Leverage

One of the biggest mistakes I see people make in their journey to success is they try to do it all themselves. I often hear, "It's just easier to do it myself than to try to get someone else to do it." Then they complain about how busy they are and how they don't have enough time to accomplish anything. They act as if their time owns them instead of them owning their time. Isn't it true that the person earning $20,000 a year does so in the same 24 hours a day that the person earning $20 million a year has? So, time really isn't the issue. The real reason people are so busy and don't have enough time is that they lack an understanding of the time/productivity connection and how powerful an investment it is to collaborate with others. When you begin to leverage yourself by patiently educating and empowering others so that you can get more done, you are truly on your way to wealth.

It was the third time in a week that my six-year-old asked me to tie his shoes, and of course his requests always came at an inconvenient time when I was on the phone or involved with something else. Oh, the tragedies of working at home! I knew I had a choice: I could save time now and quickly tie his shoes in order to return to what I was doing, or I could take the time and teach him how to do it himself. After a moment of thought, I kneeled down, took his fingers in mine, and invested the time to teach him. In no time at all, I had my little man filled with pride and I realized I just taught myself one of my own lessons! I leveraged myself so that I could get more done. Now, the laces are still getting tied, just not by me. Blake learned to tie his own shoes when I learned to teach him. I *invested* my time to train someone else versus *spending* my time by doing it myself. In business, what sets the wealthy apart from everyone else is that they find ways to profit using the strategic advantage of leverage.

Here's a more visual example of how leverage works. Suppose you're a workaholic and put in 15 hours a day, 7 days a week. At this pace, it won't take long before you to start missing out on any kind of a life outside of work and eventually burn out.

15 hours   x   7 days   =   105 hours per week

Now, let's say you empower 10 other people as part of a team and each person adds just 1 hour a day to work on the project.

1 hour   x   7 days   x   10 people   =   70 hours per week

That's 70 work hours per week that you just converted into more family time! Leveraging ourselves helps us to work smarter, not harder. And the more people there are, the more leverage we possess.

You'll find that not just individuals, but smart companies are also using the power of leverage. Look around; many successful businesses are reorganizing as networks, stressing interdependent alliances and strategic partnerships with other companies rather than self-sufficiency in all areas. Airlines and credit card companies will often link up to leverage off of each others large consumer bases. The credit card company benefits by offering the added incentive of earning mileage points for using their card. At the same time, the airlines gain the loyalty of the card holder. Both entities, through a mutually beneficial arrangement, save hundreds of thousands of dollars in marketing and advertising costs, all while increasing sales and profits.

Large or small, team alliances are good for business, and finding the key contacts who possess the resources you lack is a significant step towards success. Think about this: Whatever and whoever you need to link up with to build your dream already exists! The people who possess the information, knowledge, and resources you seek are alive and breathing right now. Your job is to find them and figure out how you can successfully partner with them. With the right dream and the right team, everyone will achieve more.

First Who, Then What

Author and researcher Jim Collins says this, "First who, then what." In his book *Good to Great*, Collins studied dozens of companies for years and analyzed their differences. He found that the most successful CEOs, those who turned a bad, mediocre, or good company into a great company, all had something in common. *First*, they got the right people on the team, the wrong people off the team, the right people in the right positions–and *then* they figured out which part of the company's goals that team could tackle. When they had the right people, they took the team and the company to great success. He says, "The old adage 'People are your most important asset' turns out to be wrong. People are not your most important asset, the *right* people are. Great vision without great people is irrelevant."

The movie *Miracle* is a great example of teamwork. It's a story of how a rag tag group of young kids came together to form the U.S. Hockey team that defeated the Russians in the 1980 Olympic games. One of my favorite scenes is where the U.S. head coach is talking to one of his recruiters and says, "I'm not looking for the best players. I'm looking for the right players." He wasn't looking to find the greatest skilled players. He knew the U.S. team would never win on skill alone. What he was looking for were the players who were willing to give it their very best–players with heart and a fierce intensity to win.

THE
CURRENCY OF THE
FUTURE

"No one waxes a rented car."
–John Maxwell

You can look through stacks of impressive resumes and interview people on their qualifications all day, but until you look someone in the eye and see that flame of desire burning within them, you will never know that you've got the right player. There are tens of thousands of great people out there right now with amazing dreams and ambitions who have been overlooked, passed up, and set aside–people who, for some reason or another, just haven't found the right opportunity. Give the right person the right opportunity and they will flourish and be forever grateful for it. There is no shortage of the right people, only a shortage of people to recognize and develop the greatness in others.

Finding the *right* people also means letting go of the *wrong* people. This can be difficult to do, especially if they are close friends or family members. We all naturally desire to succeed alongside those we care about the most. But often times, those closest to us with the best of intentions can be holding us back inadvertently. Choose your travel partners wisely and ask yourself this question, "What are their motives, their values, their dreams and goals?" Are they in tune with yours? Don't waste your time with people who won't support you in your journey unless you are willing to sacrifice your dream. And make no mistake about it, there is no use trying to convince someone who has no dream that they need one. You might as well be dragging a dead horse. No matter how much money and influence your team earns, without shared values, only disappointment will result. And failure to live your values is not a setback; it is real failure.

The Art of Teamwork

What are the attributes of a winning team? What makes good teams great and how do they consistently outperform others? While having the right people can position a team for success, it doesn't guarantee great teamwork anymore than having the right colors on a palette guarantees a beautiful painting. I believe there's an art to shaping the right environment for teamwork that anyone can acquire. Put the right players in the right environment and you're bound to see an explosion!

Have you ever walked through a model home? Some of them are just breathtaking aren't they? Yet, as I walk through those homes with their perfectly matched decor, I can't help but feel that something is missing.

While the decorators certainly make the house look beautiful, it doesn't really feel like a home to me without the warmth and unique identity of a family sharing their lives within it. Just like a home, great teams come to life through their unique differences. One of my favorite quotes is by Mother Teresa; "You can do what I cannot do. I can do what you cannot do. Together, we can do great things."

I can look at one of the business teams that I'm involved with now and see that Peter's gift is interviewing; Angie's gift is product education; Ernie's strength is team communication; Scott's strength is humor and wisdom, and Chris is a great public speaker who communicates our team vision. By the way, one of the most valuable players on the team is Mary who is shy and introverted. She provides a sense of stability and makes everyone feel important because she focuses on others. Her gifts are invaluable because they create the right atmosphere for the team. Our members know and love their roles because they are using their own unique strengths. Our success has come from a well organized team of talent in its right place. There is not a superstar or a failure. We all understand that where one person is weak, there is someone else on the team who is unique.

"Synergy is the highest activity of life; it creates new untapped alternatives; it values and exploits the mental, emotional, and psychological differences between people." –Stephen Covey

Just as each person should have a clearly defined dream, a team also needs to be clear on where they are going and why. A successful team is one that beats with one heart. John Maxwell says, "Great vision precedes great accomplishment." When team members are convinced that their individual effort is contributing to a greater cause that they believe in, they will devote themselves wholly and find a greater sense of fulfillment in their work. Everyone on the team must buy into its vision. A powerful vision is not some framed statement hanging on the wall that no one pays attention to. Rather, it is a cause that stirs the passions, one that is worth working hard, sacrificing, and coming together for. It is fueled from within, not imposed from without.

Perhaps the most predominantly neglected element of teamwork is the power of empowerment. Do team members feel empowered to affect changes and make a difference through their decisions in their area of responsibility? Or, are they just a "yes man" far removed from making any real impact on the team? Micro-managers and closed-minded, controlling leaders do not empower their teams. In the movie *My Fair Lady*, linguist Professor Henry Higgins makes a bet with a friend that he can transform an impoverished flower girl with a terrible cockney accent into a well spoken lady. He succeeds, and at the end of the movie the flower girl Eliza says, "The difference between a lady and a flower girl is not how she behaves, but how she is treated."

When you trust people and set high expectations for them, they'll prove you right. On the other hand, when you baby people and insist on being involved in every aspect and detail of what they do, they'll prove you right again. Two years ago, I attended a business conference on teamwork and heard John Maxwell say, "No one waxes a rented car." I thought, "Yeah, he's right. I've never taken my AVIS rental car to a car wash." Your team will either be structured for control or for growth. Empowerment is all about ownership; people protect and nurture what is theirs. Empower your team by giving them a challenge, giving them freedom, and then giving them the credit.

It took me ten years in my business to finally discover the power of a team. Over the first several years in an i-commerce venture, I had attracted almost a dozen very bright and talented people to our organization. We used our public speaking, marketing savvy, and influence to attract others and our company skyrocketed! We were setting the pace in our industry. We had a compelling vision for growth, solid leadership, and a successful business model. To top it off, we looked good, smelled good, and talked good. We were a team destined for greatness! Then, it stagnated. We never captured the market share we had hoped for. What happened? I led the team poorly because we lacked true teamwork. The collaborative "ownership" of the rest of the team was missing. No one was waxing the car because it felt like a "rental."

A New Standard

Recently, I was at a party and one of the gals was bending the ears of half a dozen guests complaining about how long she waited on hold that afternoon with the phone company. She went on and on for over 15 minutes bragging about her problem. It turned out her argument was over a one dollar phone call. I thought to myself, "This is ridiculous! Six people just collectively endured a total of one and a half hours of her spewing over one dollar!" Six people just had their evening compromised and their attitudes sucked dry over the selfish, small thinking of one person.

I'm sure you don't need to me tell you about examples like these. Chances are, you can rewind your clock 24 hours and begin to remember all the chattering and conversation over nothing of real value. "The traffic on the freeway was terrible this morning." "Did you hear about what happened to Julie?" "Did I tell you about my car accident last week?" A majority of people spend most of their time thinking and talking about problems. Hey let's face it, it's a comfortable place to be. As Anthony Robbins suggests, "Identify your problems, but give your time and energy to solutions." People focusing on their problems are looking for sympathy and attention, but you and I can submit a new standard. Imagine how energizing and adventurous life would be if you and the people you spend time with talked about ideas, vision, and where you're headed?

The Currency of the Future will not be paid to whiners and complainers. There will be nearly one million self-made millionaires created in the next five years and I can tell you that they are engaged in higher levels of thinking and conversation. The truth is, people who are chasing their dreams can not afford to sit around and listen to people complain about their circumstances. They are committed to a higher standard and choose to engage themselves in more optimistic conversation.

What about the things we say about each other? Have you ever noticed how most TV sitcoms are based on a group of people knocking each other? Families, friends, and co-workers all cracking jokes about their shortcomings and trying to "one up" the last put down. Our society is plagued with the damaging habit of derogatory talk. Haven't we all seen

59

or heard someone ranting about how pathetic their spouse, neighbor, or co-worker is? What might happen if we made a habit of talking about and encouraging the good things in each other instead? Do you think people would feel better about themselves and others? Would there be more trust and productivity? Absolutely! Successful teams have mastered the art of edifying and uplifting one another–even behind their backs. A group becomes a team when each member is secure enough in themselves and their contribution to praise the skills of the others.

Men Die for It, Babies Cry for It

Recognition is another way of encouraging productivity in team members. So often people are recognized and credited only for failing to meet deadlines or falling short of expectations. Do you remember the last time you were criticized in front of a group of people? How did that make you feel? Humiliated, frustrated, and resentful? Now think about the last time you were recognized and praised for something well done in front of the team. How did that affect you? Were you encouraged, confident, secure, and hopeful? Were you driven to achieve even more?

Ernest Shakleton, when recruiting his team of seamen for a voyage to cross the unexplored Antarctic continent, placed an ad in the paper that read, "Men wanted for Hazardous Journey. Small wages, bitter cold, long months of complete darkness, constant danger, safe return doubtful. Honour and recognition in case of success." Who in the world would respond to an ad like that? Amazingly, thousands responded and asked to join the expedition–all for a chance to be recognized as the first to cross Antarctica.

Just for fun, try this out on a spouse, a child, or a friend to see the powerful effects of recognition. The next time you are with them, catch them doing something right or find a great quality about them and genuinely praise them for it. If you can do this in the presence of other people, even better. Just watch the expression on their face. I'll bet you make their day.

Friends of ours have a three-year-old daughter, Riley, who one day decided to play with the kitchen mop. After pushing it around the kitchen floor as she had seen her mom do, she said, "Look mommy, I cleaned the floor all up!" Her mother praised her efforts and even commented to her dad when he came home what a good job of cleaning she had done. He responded with even more lavish praise. Her eyes lit up and beamed with pride as she took her father's hand to show him where she had cleaned. Since then, she has made a habit of cleaning the floor. Grown-ups are no different from children in that we all respond best to praise and recognition.

We also all like to have fun don't we? Recently, we ran a promotion in our organization where those who met the qualifications were invited to a Luau party at our home, complete with Polynesian dancers and a roasted pig. Before long, there was a buzz on the street about the "mother of all parties" and the results were amazing! Teams got focused, set goals, and worked together to make sure that no one would miss out on this landmark event.

As silly as it seems, sometimes we'll do more just to be a part of the festivities, the good times, and plain old fun! The Luau also helped people learn to set and achieve bite size goals on the way to success. Breaking larger goals down into monthly, weekly, and daily increments gives team members an opportunity to get some wins under their belt, which boosts their confidence and belief in their ability to attain their larger goal.

Another way to help teams win is to make things competitive. Have you ever noticed how every sport has a championship, every professional industry an awards ceremony, and every school a valedictorian? I believe it's because the competitive urge is a basic part of our human nature. My mentor says it this way, "I don't know too many people who like dust and taillights." Know your players and encourage those teams and individuals who want to be a part of a healthy competition to do so. The desire to win can often mobilize a team to gel and work together like never before. It helps them to set goals and get focused on producing results.

"When a team of dedicated individuals makes a commitment to act as one... the sky's the limit." –unknown

Chapter V
Use Your Gifts

W hat energizes and excites you? What gets your creative juices flowing? I ask these questions because most people don't. People spend more time planning a vacation than they do researching their own life! I'm simply asking you to think through your life and begin to scribble down what catches your attention, what captivates you, and what takes your breath away. What have you found yourself involved in that made you forget about time?

"Your chances of success are directly proportional to the degree of pleasure you derive from what you do." –Michael Korda

Most people go through life without truly enjoying their work. For one reason or another, we begin to believe that putting aside our true desires and burying ourselves in drudgery is the only way to succeed. We become stuck in our routines and dulled by the repetitious actions until the busyness of life takes over and prevents us from taking time to think, reflect, evaluate, and make adjustments in our journey. Remember, The Currency of the Future involves *thinking* and *acting*. It is so simple that it often eludes us. Oprah Winfrey said, "The key to success is to discover what you love and find a way to offer it to others."

Each of us is endowed with a unique gift called desire. Defined as: "The natural longing that is excited by the enjoyment or the thought of any good, and impels to action or effort its continuance or possession." Your desire can lead you to accomplishing great things in life. Don't shove it under the rug and ignore it!

Another precious gift we all possess is the capacity to think. Are you using your gifts or are they still sitting nicely packaged just waiting for you to open them? When Dr. Albert Switzer was asked what is wrong with mankind today, the great doctor paused for a moment and said, "Men simply don't think." Strip away the busyness for a moment and take the time to think. It sounds silly doesn't it–take the time to think? Let me ask you this: When was the last time you actually thought through and reflected on your life? When was the last time you wrote down on paper what you enjoy doing, what you're good at, or how you could make a living doing what you love?

Henry Ford was a successful entrepreneur and a great thinker. Yet the so-called intellectual society criticized and ridiculed him as being ignorant and uneducated. Ford once filed a libel suit against one particular newspaper that had printed an editorial claiming just that. During the suit, the newspaper's attorney placed Ford on the stand. Determined to prove his ignorance, he began asking Ford a barrage of questions.

The questions he posed related to textbook facts such as fundamental principles of government, the dates of the Revolutionary War, and the identity of Benedict Arnold. Ford, becoming tired of his line of questioning, explained that if he wanted answers to those questions, he could summon any number of men who could answer them by simply pushing a button on his desk. He then turned to the attorney and asked, "Now, will you kindly tell me, why I should clutter up my mind with general knowledge, for the purpose of being able to answer questions, when I have men around me who can supply any knowledge I require?"

Ford understood that what matters most is our ability to *think*. To be able to reason, use judgement, discern, create, conceive, imagine, visualize, assimilate, and evolve. These qualities are much more valuable than having a lot of knowledge.

"Thinking is the hardest work there is. That is why so few people engage in it." –Henry Ford

Bull's-eye

Are you "cluttering your mind with general knowledge" instead of using it for its intended purpose–*to think*? Even a monkey can figure out which lane of traffic is moving faster or what channel on TV is more entertaining. You are capable of so much more! Open your precious gifts and begin to engage in your life's journey.

Here's a compelling excerpt from Jim Collins' book, *Good to Great*. The following text absolutely nails to the wall the foundation of The Currency of the Future.

> *Suppose you were able to construct a work life that meets the following three tests. First, you are doing work for which you have a genetic or God-given talent, and perhaps you could become one of the best in the world in applying that talent. ("I feel that I was just born to be doing this.") Second, you are paid for what you do. ("I get paid to do this? Am I dreaming?") Third, you are doing work you are passionate about and absolutely love to do, enjoying the actual process for its own sake. ("I look forward to getting up and throwing myself into my daily work, and I really believe in what I'm doing.")*

Look at the three questions again:
1. Am I doing work that I have a great talent for?
2. Am I paid well for what I do?
3. Am I passionate about my work?

If your answers are "slim to none," then it's time to change. Change your attitude, change your focus, or in some cases, it may be time to change your career. Maybe you have been misguided by advice like, "The secret to success in life is to work on your weaknesses." Unfortunately, focusing on your weaknesses usually only takes you from an area of incompetent to competent. Overcome what weaknesses you must so that you can position yourself to focus a majority of your time developing your very best. To summarize author Dan Sullivan, people who constantly focus on their weaknesses struggle and live lives filled with a sense of frustration, wasted potential, and missed opportunity. Conversely, those who delegate their weak and mediocre skills to others, free up their time to work in their "Best Zone" and experience a sense of simplicity, fulfillment, and clarity.

Everyone has 24 hours in a day. How you use those 24 hours will determine your overall success and fulfillment in life. The diagram below illustrates four areas in which you can spend your time. Notice that it isn't made up of typical areas like work, play, hobbies, and sleep. Most people would probably advise you to "Work harder and put more time into your career," or "Spend less time on your hobbies and go get a degree," or "You need to get more balance in your life." While there may be some merit to their comments, their advice is off target.

Your success or failure is more dependent upon how much time you spend in each of the zones: Incompetent, Competent, Good, and Best. Average people spend most of their time in the areas of Incompetent, Competent, or Good, while the most successful people spend a majority of their lives in their Best zone, in the "bull's-eye," doing what they are great at. Here again, The Currency of the Future involves *thinking*. You can't go through life a "wandering generality," yet expect to be rewarded. Extraordinary achievement will come from discovering and applying your genius. Ask people who are close to you what they see as a strength or talent in your life. Then ask yourself: What skills am I regularly complemented on? What do I do best? What do I enjoy? How can I position myself to spend most of my time in the bull's-eye?

THE CURRENCY OF THE FUTURE

"There is no dirty work, just the wrong person doing the wrong work."

—Brad DeHaven

"Success is waking up in the morning, whoever you are, wherever you are, however old or young, and bounding out of bed because there's something out there that you love to do, that you believe in, that you're good at–something that's bigger than you are, and you can hardly wait to get at it again today." –Whit Hobbs

A Masterpiece

Doing what you love and what gives you a sense of purpose simplifies your life and therefore concentrates your abilities; and concentration adds power. It is like the compass that guides you along the way. Those without it are pulled in every direction and each simple step forward becomes a complex decision. They experience confusion and anxiety while trying to determine where they should go and what they should do next. In contrast, those who rely on a steady compass are free from distractions and able to confidently advance in the pursuit of their ultimate goal. Every step is in line with their intended purpose allowing them to have fun and enjoy the journey rather than fear it. Great productivity, confidence, growth, fulfillment, and creativity will result from using your unique abilities. It is what will ultimately bring you great success.

"Where there is no hope in the future, there is no power in the present."
–John Maxwell

My father-in-law was a successful attorney for over 30 years. Three years ago, he and my mother-in-law took a vacation to Santa Fe, New Mexico where they toured through several bronze galleries. As they browsed from sculpture to sculpture, the unique beauty of each piece captivated him and amplified his lifelong desire to try his own hand at sculpting. When he returned home, at age 62, he made the decision to pursue his dream. He has since studied under a master sculptor and gone on to create a bronze bust of a famous artist which is now located in a museum. He enjoys every minute of his work while achieving thousands of dollars in sales, all from the decision to uncover a unique gift he always had within him. It is never too late to start in the direction of your dream, to change your course and discover your true potential.

Recognizing the gifts in others is equally as important as using our own. I have a couple of business partners who handle all the scheduling and hosting responsibilities for the out-of-town guests that come in to speak to our organization. Bob and his wife care for every guest as if they were the president, and they are the best hosts on the planet because they love to take care of others. Because of their wonderful gift, taking extra special care of our guests' needs and making sure they are comfortable comes naturally to them, and it's something they enjoy doing. Recognizing their gift and positioning them to apply it in a way that contributes to the organization, in turn makes them feel valued. It's a win-win situation. Conversely, I've seen others on our team who groan at this responsibility and take it on with no enthusiasm whatsoever. The result? No one is happy! Michael Gerber says in his book, *The E-Myth*, "The problem is not that the owners of small businesses in the country don't work; the problem is that they're doing the wrong work."

Believe it or not, some people actually love making and analyzing spreadsheets! They are energized and excited when they're working with data. Others grow dizzy and tired just looking at them. Take a look at where you work. Do you see people who are exhausted at the end of the day? I bet you could pinpoint those who are grudgingly doing the *wrong* work. You may want to loan them a copy of this book! Now, look around and think about those who are excited and energized. They're the ones who are smiling and enjoying their work most of the time. These people are probably using their gifts and feeling valued.

"When love and skill work together, expect a masterpiece."
–John Ruskin

THE
CURRENCY OF THE
FUTURE

"There is a time when we must
firmly choose the course we will follow,
or the relentless drift of events
will make the decisions for you."
—Herbert V. Prochnow

Chapter VI
Stay the Course

Success requires learning, changing, and growing. Most people never find success because they think it's a medal around their neck, capturing a flag, or discovering the Holy Grail. Others believe it is a relationship to be won, a position to be earned, or an object to be possessed. It's none of those things. I've heard it said that, "Success doesn't happen in a day, it happens daily." Success is not a destination to be reached. It is a process–a journey, and you do it one mile at time, one day at time.

Look at the number of movie stars, singers, and professional athletes who have earned huge fortunes during their careers, yet end up penniless, heavily in debt, or bankrupt. And what about people who have inherited their fortunes? Figures show that in most cases, by the time the second inheriting generation passes on, there is only 10 percent of it left. The same goes for lottery winners where nearly one-third are bankrupt within a few short years. Accumulating large sums of money does not make you a success. A truly successful person, though they lose it all, could build it back up again–because genuine wealth is within the person, not their fortunes.

Developing your wealth, your Currency of the Future requires that you stay the course. In the film *The Patriot*, the lead character, Benjamin Martin, is a father torn between protecting his family and fighting for his nation. When a British officer murders his son in front of his very own eyes, he realizes he no longer has a choice. His reason becomes clear and he joins a grass roots movement to fight for the freedom of his family and his nation. At one point, after the unthinkable death of his two sons and the crippling losses of his militia, he begins to break down and succumb to defeat. A Continental officer attempts to persuade him not to quit the cause. "Stay the course, Martin. Stay the course." But Martin, overcome by his grief replies, "I've run the course." Later, as he begins to load his dead son's personal belongings on his horse, he finds an American flag that his son had affectionately restored. The flag reminds him of his reason, his purpose, and ultimately puts him back in the fight to stay the course.

What's your course? In order to stay the course, there needs to be a course. If you're not sure of your course, trust me, you don't have one. If you were clear on your course, you'd know exactly where you were going and what you were doing today, this week, this month, and this year. Think about it: If you were going to take a two-week family vacation, wouldn't you spend some time planning it? Do you think you might look at a map to see where you are going? Would you know how you were going to get there and how long it might take? Well, this isn't a two-week vacation, it's your life! Anyone can stick it out in times of growth and prosperity on sincere interest alone, but when adversity comes knocking on your door, you had better know your reason. Your dream is where you will find the reserve necessary to sustain you through the difficult times. Without it, you're roadkill.

"Going To" vs. "Going Through"

Staying the course means that you can't afford to major on the minors. On your journey to your best life, it's essential that you focus on the MAJORS. One of my favorite parting words with my friends and business partners is, "Keep Chargin'!" It's short for "Keep charging forward, stay the course, keep focused on the majors!" I sign most of my e-mails the same way. Instead of Sincerely, Cheers, and Kind Regards, I prefer to sign, "Keep Chargin'!" because that person may be facing rejection, doubt, fear, or heartache that day. They may be questioning whether or not they have what it takes to ever reach their dreams. "Keep Chargin'!" is my way of saying, "You've got what it takes. Stay focused and you'll make it."

You're probably thinking, "Yeah, but you don't know my situation. It is a MAJOR and there's no getting around it." You're right. It probably is a MAJOR because you choose to make it one. For every set of circumstances or failed effort you point to, I can show you others who faced greater obstacles, tougher circumstances, and more devastating setbacks, yet managed to overcome them and achieve their dreams in spite of it all. What are your reasons, your dreams? What are you willing to fight for? Who are you wanting to win for? What do you want to have, do, and become? Those are the MAJORs in your life.

Look at the "Personal Focus" illustration below. You'll notice that there are two concentric circles. The larger circle is titled **"What I'm going through"** and contains all the things in life that you are going through right now: problems, concerns, worries, all the things that are holding you back. This is the circle that most people major on. Winston Churchill said, "A pessimist sees the difficulty in every opportunity; an optimist sees the opportunity in every difficulty." A lot of folks like to moan and groan about how big their "going through" circle is. In fact, I know people that actually like to brag about their "going through" circle. They showcase their negative circumstances as if they were medals around their neck. Personally, I can hardly stand a moment with people like this. They are a total drag to be around–they suck the life right out of you. A friend once told me, "You can make excuses or you can make money, but you can't make both."

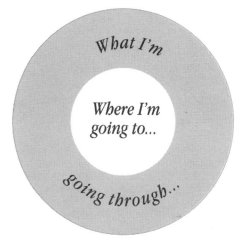

The center circle titled **"Where I'm going to"** should be the real focus in our lives. It represents our true calling and the things we are meant to accomplish. The inner circle contains the answers to the question, "What would you do with your life if you knew you couldn't fail?"

One of the greatest visionaries of the twentieth century was Walt Disney. He created the first cartoon with sound, the first all-color cartoon, and the first full-length animated feature film. Although he never lived to see it through, his greatest masterpiece was Disneyland. After he died, a Disney executive and several reporters were hovering over the massive park in Anaheim, California that is now Disneyland. One of the reporters said, "It's too bad that Walt never saw this." Without missing a beat, the Disney executive said, "He did see this, and that's why it's here." For Walt Disney, vision was never a problem. He painted the picture of Disneyland in his mind and ignited the hearts and imagination of others to complete the project. Because of his creativity and focus on where he was going, he always saw what *could* be. If you lack vision, look inside yourself and draw on your natural gifts and desires. Look to your calling if you have one. And if you still struggle defining your center circle, then consider hooking up with a leader whose vision resonates with you.

The Currency of the Future will be paid to those who spend the MAJORity of their time in the inner circle. So many people never find success because they major on the minors (the outer circle). They focus on things that are ultimately insignificant to the big picture. "I have to pay my bills, run these errands, deal with this problem, answer the phone..." You know, the day-to-day stuff that sidetracks us. No one ever really plans to be unsuccessful in life. They start off with high hopes and big dreams, but something happens along the way. Their convictions to change the world downgrade to commitments to pay the bills; rather than make a difference, they make a salary, and rather than look forward, they look back. Why? Because they get so caught up in the minors that they fail to notice that their life is passing them by–until it is too late.

Let's do a quick exercise. Fill in all the problems, excuses, circumstances, and challenges that you are going through in your life right now. Go ahead, have a blast! List all the things that are holding you back, your problems, everything. Write them all in the big gray circle.

74

Now that that's out of the way, you have a choice. You can either major on your circumstances and your problems and stay where you are, or you can minimize them with a powerful inner circle. If you continuously focus on what you are going through, your inner circle will keep shrinking and shrinking until it is completely overshadowed by your problems. Don't let your circumstances consume your inner circle (what you truly want) to the point that you are left feeling like, "There's nothing I can do. It's hopeless." Your thinking and skewed perceptions of reality are what makes a situation hopeless. Change your thinking and you change your reality. I often say, "If you continue to do what you've always done, you'll continue to have what you've always had." Focusing on your problems keeps you there.

Auto-pilot

How can we change our thinking? Reading this book is a great start! Another way is to change what you say to yourself. Have you ever stopped to really think about the things you say? Do you ever say things like...

"I'm set in my ways."
"I'm too old to change."
"I can't do that."
"It won't work."

Do you realize that these kinds of statements are hindering your success? Once you make a statement like that, you've basically turned your mind off. You've given yourself permission to stop thinking and looking for a solution or a possibility. The tongue has appropriately been compared to the rudder of a ship. Though it may seem like an insignificantly small instrument, it has the power to steer the course of the entire vessel.

Dr. Martin Seligman of the University of Pennsylvania spent more than 25 years studying people who held the belief that they were incapable of improving their lives. His research showed that the most common manifestation of their helplessness was contained in the two words "I can't." When offered an opportunity, they all had some sort of a self-limiting reason that immediately slammed on the brakes of their potential and short-circuited any attempt or desire to change.

When I first began building my i-commerce business, our volume grew steadily until it seemed to plateau for over a year. I would tell my wife things like, "I just can't get out of this funk." "We're stuck with negative cashflow." "Why can't I get it to work the way it should?" Little did I know how powerful these statements were. I was regularly speaking negative confessions to myself and those around me.

As my mentor learned of my discouraging thoughts and damaging self talk, he taught me this vital lesson: "Don't let the words of your mouth destroy the work of your hands." He led me to a classic audio titled *The Strangest Secret* by Earl Nightingale. I listened to the audio over and over again. It became one of the major turning points in my journey.

It taught me that our subconscious minds, like a computer hard drive, can be programmed by our thoughts and speech. As we program our subconscious, it then goes about the task of running the program as instructed, regardless of what our conscious mind may be doing. Another way of looking at it is to see our subconscious mind as the auto-pilot function of a boat. It automatically steers the boat in the direction it has been programmed for. Depending upon the years of programming that has been entered into our subconscious mind, our boat is either headed for failure, success, or somewhere in between.

Our conscious mind acts as the manual override and allows us to steer the boat in a new direction. But as soon as we stop consciously steering the boat, the auto-pilot takes over again and veers it back to its original course. It is a continually conflicting struggle for control until the auto-pilot is reprogrammed to match the course of the conscious mind. What is important to understand is that the auto-pilot has no personal preference of its own to head in any particular direction. It is a tool, one that can be your greatest ally or your worst enemy.

Reprogramming the subconscious mind is not a difficult task by any means. It's actually very simple to do, but it requires time and consistency. The subconscious doesn't replace information, it assimilates it. Therefore it's impossible to change all that it has learned with one new thought or experience. Think of it as red food coloring. It takes more than a couple drops of water to make it clear. But as you continue to add more water, drop by drop, it grows clearer and clearer. And if you eventually added enough drops, it would become completely clear even though it still contained the red food coloring in it.

Feed your subconscious mind daily with information that will reprogram it in the direction of your success. Feed it with new thoughts, new experiences, and consciously choose to speak new words and ask yourself the right questions.

When we ask ourselves a question, our brain searches through the files in our mind to come up with an answer. It's just like Google, the popular Internet search engine, except it's faster and more efficient. But just like Google, your mind will only answer the questions you ask it. In place of the previous statements, try these on for size...

"What am I willing to change for?"
"What do I want to do with my life and how can I
fit it in to the time I have?"
"How can I do that?"
"How can it work?"

Can you see the difference in your thought process? These questions position your thinking within the realm of possibilities. Remember, what we say has the power to change not only our thoughts, but also the course of our future. Replace words like "never," "can't," "but," and "won't" with more productive words like "when," "how," "why," and "will." Make it a habit to be conscious of the words you speak and ask yourself the right questions.

Now, let's get back to your circle. Think of one thing, one key thing to put into your inner circle. Think of something specific that you are passionate about. Something you've always dreamed of accomplishing. What would make a difference in your life? What allows you to see beyond your circumstances, even if it's just for a moment? It doesn't matter how spectacular it is, or how small it is. Just think of one thing and write it in your "going to" circle. One thing that draws your focus and your attention to your inner circle. Do it now.

If you wrote "Make more money," that's a good start. Consider what you wrote and see if it can be clarified with more detail. Your inner circle cannot be vague and it should stir up some emotion when you read it. You have to be specific and extremely clear about where you are going. Write something like, "I will be the first in a line of generations to break the cycle of poverty in our family by earning $250,000 a year." I want you to write down a total of three things in your inner circle. They can be in the area of your finances, your family, your health, or anything else that is important to you. When your circle is complete, keep it in a place where you will see it daily. Read, refresh, revisit, and rewrite your inner circle as frequently as you need to combat the inevitable "what I'm going through" reminders that you face daily.

VAGUE	CLEAR & SPECIFIC
Make more money	I will be the first in a line of generations to break the cycle of poverty in our family by earning $250,000 a year.
Have more free time	I will have the financial freedom to retire on my 30th birthday.
Travel	I will take a helicopter tour along the Na Pali coastline in Kauai and spend two weeks relaxing at the Princeville Hotel.

One of the things Kim and I have done is to make our home a storybook of the future rather than one of the past. I sketched a picture of what our property will look like in the future with palm trees, rock pool, Jacuzzi, waterfalls, and a swim up bar under a palapa. Occasionally, when a friend drops by, I ask them if they've seen the resort in my back yard. Their surprised response is usually "No" as they curiously peer out the window to see my resort. I point them to the wall instead and show them an artist's rendering of the plans. I watch their expression to see the light go on in their mind. What does your home tell the story of? Is it a story only of the past or does it also tell the tale of tomorrow?

"The biggest reason men fail is broken focus." –Mike Murdock

Stop. Before reading any further, did you actually go through and do the exercise or are you just going to skim past it? Are you really willing to leave your dreams behind that easily? No way! If you didn't do it, go back and do it! To really change and redirect the course of your life, you have to think about and apply the words of this book, not just read them.

Most people live average, routine lives because they don't want to bother with anything beyond the grind they're in. They dislike what they're doing, yet are unwilling to change. Those that do try to change often jump from one thing to the next, always looking for an easier way. They

79

THE
CURRENCY OF THE
FUTURE

"**Make your home a storybook of the future rather than one of the past.**"
–Brad DeHaven

Make A Wish Foundation
one million and 00/100

spend their time in vain trying this and that, never truly committing themselves to any one thing. Why? Why is it that so many people live lives short of their true potential? I believe that it's partly because we're so conditioned to expect instant gratification. We live in a microwave society where everything is at our convenience. If we want something now, we get it. And if we're made to wait too long, we go somewhere else and get it. It's no wonder we expect success to arrive instantly after our first attempts.

The wake up call is this: Success is not something you're going to stumble upon or happen to find out there. It is something to be developed within you. There will be many obstacles to overcome in the process of becoming the success you truly long to be, but challenges in the pursuit of what you love, your dream, are bearable. They're no more difficult to manage than a lifetime of doing what you dislike. They're just part of the journey.

The Duck Pond

A few years ago, my wife and I were shooting for a significant goal in our business. It was a big stretch for us because it depended on the collaborative efforts of several teams over a six month period. By helping each team accomplish their goals, we would in turn achieve ours. We believed that with focused work and effort, each team could be positioned for success, so we entered into the endeavor wholeheartedly. Then shortly after the second month, I got a phone call from one of my key players. He called to tell me that he was facing unexpected challenges in his life and that he would have to quit the team. The rest of the conversation drowned out as my disappointment overcame me. I hung up the phone, hurled it at the wall as hard as I could and watched it shatter to a hundred pieces. Then I screamed at the top of my lungs, "Bring it on!"

Over the next couple of months, things started to fall apart. It was as if somewhere inside of me, the goal had died. My focus had shifted from the goal to my circumstances and I began contemplating the possibility that it just wasn't going to happen. Right about that time, we attended a business conference along with many of the top leaders in our industry. While we were backstage, we overheard someone ask which venue would be the location for our next conference. The response was, "It's at the uh, pond? The duck pond?" Then I heard, "Yeah, the Duck Pond. It's in Anaheim, California."

I still get shivers up my spine thinking about it today because for years prior to that, I had painted a picture in my mind and had shared a vision with our team that we would someday fill the Duck Pond arena and hold our conferences there. The conference they were discussing was where my wife, myself, and each team leader would be recognized if we all achieved our goals. Almost immediately, my mind started to refocus. It was at that point that I became convinced beyond a shadow of a doubt that it was a done deal. Four months later, we were each recognized on stage in front of an arena full of people at the Duck Pond, just as we had envisioned it.

I've heard it said that circumstances do not make us, they reveal our true character to ourselves and to others. How will you choose to handle your challenges? Will you cower in the face of adversity or will you come back stronger than ever? One thing is certain, you will never discover what you are made of by quitting on a worthy goal. Every ship is believed to be seaworthy as it sits in the safety of the harbor, but no one will ever know its true strength and character until it weathers the storms in the open sea. We can either rise up to meet adversity head on, or we can run from it. These are our defining moments in life.

Christopher Columbus could have turned his ships around after any one of the difficulties his crew faced. His name would not be known to us today if he had. But he was a dreamer. He had a gut instinct that they would succeed and he was willing to boldly risk defeat for the chance to discover a New World. Throughout his journey he wrote in his diary by candlelight. Each night, each entry described hardship, famine, disappointment, challenges, and setbacks. But there were five words that remained constant by his pen each night... *"This day we sailed on."*

This day through hardship... we sailed on.
This day through famine... we sailed on.
This day though plagued by doubt and disbelief... we sailed on.

82

"I will do today what other people won't so that I can have tomorrow what other people won't." –unknown

Success Lies on the Other Side of Failure

Success is there for the taking, but its treasure is often guarded by a rugged terrain riddled by the pitfalls of failure and adversity. Though its path seems intimidating, the way is opened to those that are determined enough to persevere after others have turned back. It is what we do after we fail, lose, and get knocked down that counts. If we want to achieve more than what the average person achieves, then we must persist longer than the average person is willing to persist. Where others are not willing to go is where we will find the greatest treasures of all.

"Only a man who knows what it is like to be defeated can reach down to the bottom of his soul and come up with the extra ounce of power it takes to win when the match is even." –Muhammad Ali

Born in Manitoba, Canada, Terry Fox was just like any other teenage boy. He was involved in many sports, loved spending time with his friends, and was optimistic about his future. Then at only eighteen years of age, he was diagnosed with bone cancer and forced to have his right leg amputated. While he was in the hospital, Terry was so overcome by the suffering of other cancer patients, many of them young children, that he felt a responsibility to make a difference. Inspired by a magazine article about an amputee who had run in the New York marathon, Terry decided he would run across Canada to raise $1 million for cancer research.

Two years after his operation, Terry began training to prepare for what he called "The Marathon of Hope." He trained for 15 months, ran a total of 3,159 miles, and ran for 101 consecutive days. He continued to run even when his stump was raw and bleeding so that he could get up to 23 miles a day. His mother thought he was crazy and when Terry approached the Canadian Cancer Society about his run, they doubted his success and told him to go and earn some seed money and to find corporate sponsors. They believed they'd never hear from Terry Fox again.

83

But Terry was determined. He earned several sponsors and set off on the greatest adventure of his life. He ran 26 miles a day through ice storms, bitter winds, and summer heat, through fishing villages and large cities. "I loved it," Terry said. "People thought I was going through hell. Maybe I was partly, but still I was doing what I wanted and a dream was coming true and that, above everything else, made it all worthwhile to me. How many people do something they really believe in? I just wish people would realize that anything's possible, if you try; dreams are made, if people try."

Enthusiasm grew and the people of Canada began latching on to Terry's dream evident by the donations that were pouring in. People would wait for hours on the roadside to watch Terry pass and sometimes a stranger would press a $100 bill into his hand as he ran by. Others would shout "Keep going, don't give up, you can do it, you can make it, we're all behind you!"

On September 1st, after 143 days and 3,339 miles, Terry was forced to stop running outside of Thunder Bay, Ontario. Cancer had appeared in his lungs and he physically could not continue to run. An entire nation was stunned and saddened, many even offered to finish the run in his place. A few short months later, Terry passed away just one month shy of his 23rd birthday. It was a journey that would never be forgotten and one that did not end with his death. To date, more than $360 million has been raised worldwide for cancer research in Terry's name through the annual Terry Fox Run held across Canada and around the world. Terry also received numerous awards and honors as well as being named in the *Guinness Book of World Records* as top fundraiser.

"Every adversity, every failure, every heartache carries with it the seed of an equal or greater benefit." –Napoleon Hill

How about you? Have you been setback or knocked down? Have you failed? Have you lost hope? Hey, let's face it; life has not been fair to any of us. We've all had challenges and disappointments. What matters is that we get back up. The human spirit that you've been endowed with is stronger than you think. You have what it takes to pull through. Find someone that overcame what you are struggling with and let them inspire you. Read about them, learn from them, and adopt their attitudes.

You may never become a history maker, a world class athlete, or a great inventor. But every one of us can achieve a measure of success if we stay the course and never let defeat have the last word.

Cripple him, and you have a Sir Walter Scott.
Lock him in a prison cell, and you have a John Bunyan.
Bury him in the snows of Valley Forge, and you have a George Washington.
Raise him in abject poverty, and you have an Abraham Lincoln.
Subject him to bitter religious prejudice, and you have a Disraeli.
Afflict him with asthma as a child, and you have a Theodore Roosevelt.
Stab him with rheumatic pains until he can't sleep without an opiate, and you have a Steinmetz.
Put him in a grease pit of a locomotive roundhouse, and you have a Walter P. Chrysler.
Make him play second fiddle in an obscure South American orchestra, and you have a Toscanini.
At birth, deny her the ability to see, hear, and speak, and you have a Helen Keller.
–From a column in "Dear Abby"

THE
CURRENCY OF THE
FUTURE

"Freedom is only part of the story and half the truth... That is why I recommend that the Statue of Liberty on the East Coast be supplanted by a Statue of Responsibility on the West Coast."

–Victor Frankl, *Man's Search for Meaning*

Chapter VII
Take Responsibility

The first of the Seven Keys was to define your reason. Have you? What is your reason? Now it's time to become personally responsible for making it a reality. In order to harness the power within The Currency of the Future, you must understand that everything that is going to happen to you for the rest of your life is up to you. You are in charge of your life.

The fact is, we don't get in life what we wish for, nor do we get what is fair. We get in life what we take responsibility for.

> You are responsible for your thoughts.
> You are responsible for your actions.
> You are responsible for your habits.
> You are responsible for your life.

Some of us have already come to terms with this understanding; others have not. I've met many "adults" in their 40s and 50s who are still blaming their circumstances and other people for their problems. Maturity doesn't come with age, it comes with the acceptance of responsibility. Those adults never really matured and unfortunately, their lives are a reflection of it.

As long as we continue to see ourselves as victims to our circumstances, we remain powerless to change. When something doesn't go as expected, our natural tendency is to blame someone else. In doing so, we lose a tremendous learning opportunity and give someone else power over the situation. Blame the government, blame your parents, blame your spouse, blame the school system... The moment you blame someone or something else, you have totally lost control of your life. For example, "If my boss hadn't changed my commission structure, I wouldn't be in this situation." True as it may be, this statement gives your boss power over the situation. You have nothing to learn and your energy is focused on blaming rather than finding a solution.

Is it easier to change the government, your parents, your spouse, the school system, and everyone else, or is it easier to change yourself? This reminds me of a story that I heard about a man who had been married seven times. He could never seem to find the right woman so he went to see a counselor to get some advice. When the counselor asked him what his past seven wives had in common, the man thought for a while, then began naming a laundry list of faults. He was certain the counselor was helping him to learn what to avoid in a future wife until he heard the counselor reply, "No, *you* are what they all had in common." What this wise counselor understood is that a successful marriage isn't finding the right person–it's being the right person. Live life as if you are the only one who will ever change.

"The best day of your life is the one on which you decide your life is your own. No apologies or excuses. No one to lean on, rely on, or blame. The gift of life is yours; ...and you alone are responsible for the quality of it." –Dan Zadra

Not only does accepting responsibility affect us, it affects the lives of those around us. Several years ago, while I was focused on expanding my business, I was averaging four to five nights a week on long distance trips away from home. Our three children at the time were all under the age of five and quite a handful for Kim as you can imagine. One night, after I had been home for several days, Kim remarked how nice it was to have me around and involved with the kids. She had been feeling alone and overworked from carrying the burden herself. And while I knew that my busy schedule had put a strain on our home, I felt driven, and perhaps somewhat justified by the fact that I was paying the price for our success.

That night, after I had read the kids a bedtime story and tucked them into bed, Kim said to me, "When you read to the kids, they grow. When you're here, good things happen. When I saw you bathing the kids last night, I felt such strong feelings towards you, it was almost like I felt physical desire for you just watching you spending that time with the kids." I realized then that I had been neglecting my responsibility as a husband and a father, and it was affecting all of us. I learned a valuable lesson that night that has stayed with me ever since. I also started bathing the kids every chance I had!

Our Inner Dialogue

Taking responsibility for what we do and what we say is an important step, but one that must be preceded by taking responsibility in our own thoughts. Our exterior life is a mere reflection of the inner dialogue that goes on in our mind. What kind of inner dialogue are you having with yourself?

Let's take a look at an example: Mark recently read an amazing book called *The Currency of the Future* and has decided to develop a new Internet business with his friend John. They come up with an initial client list and Mark makes all the calls to set up their first few appointments for the week. Most of the clients he talks to express an interest and say they would be available to meet. But as Mark and John arrive for each appointment, they grow increasingly frustrated at the fact that most of their prospective clients aren't even there! And the ones who are there say they are too busy to meet and will have to put it off until some other time. Not one scheduled appointment is kept.

Mark is furious and begins to think, "I can't believe they weren't there and didn't even have the courtesy to call and cancel! They said they would be available–they lied! Bunch of liars. I wouldn't want them as clients anyway!" After some more fuming, Mark begins to think, "Why did I ever listen to John? He told me we could make it big. What does he know about business anyway? I can't believe he got me into this situation. That's the last time I trust him. What am I going to say now when people ask me how my business is going? I'll tell them it wasn't really my idea. I was just trying to help John out."

Rather than accepting responsibility for the outcome of his meeting, Mark crafted a series of justifications. In his own thoughts, he chose to believe that he had been lied to and betrayed by a friend. He also began convincing himself that it was never his idea and that he was only trying to help John. Notice how Mark allowed his emotions to dictate his thoughts. As discussed in Chapter II, our emotional intelligence (EQ) plays a significant role in our overall success in life.

Are any of Mark's thoughts based on reality? Possibly. Is it also possible that the clients had a good reason for not being available and there really was great potential for their business? Sure. In reality, the only thing we do know is that Mark's thoughts were based on assumptions and self-preservation; not truth. The scary thing about it is that Mark will accept his destructive thoughts as truth and continue to operate in life based on those beliefs.

"It has always been a mystery to me, why people spend so much time deliberately fooling themselves by creating alibis to cover their weaknesses. If used differently, this same time would be sufficient to cure the weakness, then no alibis would be needed."
–Elbert Hubbard

What if Mark had taken responsibility in his thoughts instead? What would his inner dialogue have looked like? Perhaps he would have thought, "Why am I justifying myself? Why am I getting angry? I made those calls; what did I miss? Could I have done something different to change the outcome? What can I learn from this that will help me have more success next time? Maybe I can talk to John. I wonder what he thinks I could have done better. Maybe I didn't find and express their benefit in meeting with us. What could have happened if I had qualified their interest before scheduling the appointment."

Notice how this time, every one of Mark's thoughts leads to self-improvement rather than self-preservation. He is taking responsibility and looking for ways to have success in the future. Think of what Mark's next encounter with John and other clients would look like in each scenario. Can you see how Mark's actions in the future will be profoundly affected by the thoughts he chooses to think?

Let's look at another possibility. Same scenario, but this time Mark thinks to himself, "I should have known that no one would want to meet with us. I never do anything right. John must think I'm a total loser. I bet those clients think I'm stupid to think that I could ever earn their business."

In this case, Mark's thoughts are based on self-destructive assumptions and he will operate out of fear of failure and rejection for the rest of his life if he doesn't learn to change his thinking. Taking responsibility in his thoughts this time might look something like this: "Why am I having a pity party? What is my dream and why am I doing this? Why am I worthy of my dream? What can I do to overcome my fears and build confidence?"

Mark's thoughts now lead to self-improvement and shifts his focus from his fears to his dream. What does your inner dialogue look like? Are you taking responsibility or are you justifying yourself and blaming others? How is that affecting your success in business and in life?

"Things do not change; we change." –Henry David Thoreau

Understand that you are the only one that has the power to change your thoughts and your destiny. Those who don't take responsibility and control their thoughts will have their thoughts control their actions, and consequently, the direction of their life. For the person who has no compelling reason or desire to change, that's okay. But as a business owner, your survival will depend on your ability to find solutions. When there is a lack of results, you are responsible–it is *your* business that will fail without it.

You're either going to be disciplined from within, or you'll end up being disciplined by a boss for the rest of your life. The brief amount of time it takes to adopt successful habits is far less agonizing than living a lifetime of regrets. Having only short-term vision and satisfying the desire to live the "easy life" today neglects the consequences of tomorrow. My mentor always says, "Be temporarily ambitious so that you can be lazy first class." Develop long-term vision and decide to be personally disciplined today in return for a first rate, "easy life" tomorrow.

"You cannot escape the responsibility of tomorrow by evading it today." –Abraham Lincoln

When Mark blamed his circumstances, regardless of whether it was a conscious decision or not, he made a choice to follow the path of failure. The owner of a large chain of stores once said, "Give me the president of a company who waits for circumstances to be right and in 5 years I'll give you a stock clerk. But give me a stock clerk who makes his circumstances right and in 5 years I'll give you the president of a company." He understood that people who are answerable for their own life, no matter where they may begin, have the capacity to create the circumstances they desire to achieve their dream.

Are you still blaming someone or something from the past for hindering your success? How can you change that so that you are in control? One of my favorite quotes is, "The past does not equal the future." The past doesn't matter. What matters is what you do in the next 24 hours. Let me ask you this: Would you agree if I said that it is possible for you in the next 24 hours to do something to completely destroy your life? Sure, you could drive off a cliff or commit a crime. Then wouldn't it follow that in the next 24 hours it is possible for you to do something constructive that could completely set the course of your life in a positive new direction? Absolutely! You see, whether we like to admit it or not, we truly are in control of our thoughts, actions, and ultimately our lives. Too many people are looking in the rear-view mirror to guide themselves into the future. It's time to rip off the rear-view mirror and throw it out! Let's focus on the road map of possibilities. The currency of the past is behind us.

Employee Mentality vs. Business Owner Responsibility

The moment we take full responsibility, we are in control to impact our lives, the lives of those around us, and the course of our business. If you have been an employee your whole life, you may have to shift your thinking from employee mentality to business owner responsibility. Learning to succeed as a personal business owner is very different from "making it" as an employee. An employee's development and performance is often seen as someone else's responsibility; in your own business, it's *your* responsibility and you are the one in control. Only you can decide to invest time, money, and effort to improve yourself and learn new skills essential for building your own business.

Shifting your habits from being told what to do and what is expected of you, to determining what needs to be done and doing it is a core element of becoming a business owner. As an employee, you are accountable to a boss and a paycheck. As a business owner, you are accountable to yourself–and sometimes, we're not quite as demanding of ourselves, especially if there isn't a huge financial loss at stake. As a business owner, the good news is that you're in business for yourself, and the bad news is that you're in business for yourself. It all depends on you.

Exceptional achievers, whether they are business owners or employees, possess a unique attitude that sets them apart from the average performers in their field. They take ownership and "wax the car" even if it is not their own. They have a sense of pride about their work and care about the company or organization's success as if it were their own. They understand that what they do have ownership of is their performance and their contribution.

As a business owner, we don't have the luxury of saying things like, "That's not in my job description." "That's not my fault." "I just want to relax this weekend, maybe I can skip out on the meeting." These attitudes may not affect your paycheck as an employee, but they will certainly limit your profitability as a business owner. Many employees have only a mild interest in learning and applying themselves in their jobs, and they can often get away with it. Mild interest as a business owner will net you a hobby; and hobbies don't make you money, they cost you.

Why is it that so many businesses fail every year? It's because most people lack the responsibility to follow through on their commitments. It's just like the thousands of people who start out each New Year with a gym membership and great intentions. Their initial enthusiasm carries them through several weeks of committed workouts, and as they begin to look and feel better, they become excited about the progress they've made. Then life happens. Something comes up and they miss a workout or two. And old habits sure do have a way of settling back in quickly don't they? What happens next? Without the same excitement of starting something new, and now with a very real understanding of the effort involved, they somehow never make it back for the next workout. They lose focus, decide to put it off, and ultimately shirk their responsibility to improve themselves.

Character is doing what you said you'd do, long after the feeling has left you. And responsibility is understanding that no one is going to make your business succeed, except you. The initial enthusiasm will leave you, I can promise you that. So what are you going to do in advance to make sure that you keep going when you don't feel like it? My mentor always said that you need to protect yourself against yourself. He understood that most of us have a tendency to be lazy, so he suggested making a habit of booking your calendar two weeks in advance. Keeping pre-existing appointments takes less effort than having to set up new ones. And effectively prioritizing and scheduling your time in advance is much easier than having to rethink what needs to be done daily. Believe it or not, The Currency of the Future isn't going to just fall into your lap; you will have to take responsibility for it.

THE CURRENCY OF THE FUTURE

FUTURE

"You will either take responsibility for your
life or take orders the rest of your life."
–Robert Kiyosaki

Chapter VIII
Ignore the Critics

The moment you begin your journey to your best life, expect to be criticized. The whole purpose of learning The Currency of the Future is for you to follow and realize your dream. Throughout history, the one thing that has remained consistent among achievers is that they were laughed at, ridiculed, questioned, and misunderstood.

"To avoid criticism, be nothing, do nothing, and say nothing."
–Elbert Hubbard

So, how can we learn to manage criticism? We all want to be understood and accepted don't we? Of course! Then how can we, in our minds, reconcile the criticism we face without giving in to it? Why not start by convincing yourself first. In other words, invest in developing your belief. Ask yourself, are you sold out to your dream, your cause, and your purpose? Do you believe that what you are doing is right and good? Belief is one of those pass or fail things. You either have it or you don't. If you believe in it and your head can hit the pillow at night knowing that you're doing what's right, then that's what really matters. Critics may say this and that, but in the end, you are the one that has to live your life, not them. Make it one that you lived for what *you* believe in.

Here's a typical scenario of what happens to so many people on their journey to success:

Average Joe is an average guy who becomes inspired by his mentor Successful Scott and decides to change his life and move in the direction of his dream. He boldly steps out onto the path leading to his bright new future when, along the way, he encounters his good friend Laughing Larry who asks him where he's going. When Average Joe tells him that he's on his way to his bright new future, Laughing Larry lets out a roaring belly laugh and says, "That's a good one Joe! You're kidding, right? You think you're going to make it down this path? Is that what your buddy Successful Scott told you? Come on Joe, look at you. You're average, always have been."

Somewhat disappointed by his friend's comments, Average Joe decides to brush it off and continue down the path. Next, he runs into his brother-in-law, Critical Craig. When asked exactly where he is going, Average Joe again explains that he is on his way to his bright new future. Critical Craig crinkles his brow and replies, "You've never done anything with your life! What makes you think you're going to make it down this path? Do you have any proof or guarantee that you'll make it? And what about that friend of yours, Successful Scott. Who is he anyway? What do you really know about him? How do you know he's not lying to you? By the way, I've checked out this path myself and my understanding is that it doesn't lead anywhere. But if you think you're smarter than me, go right ahead and waste your time."

After talking to Critical Craig, Average Joe wonders to himself whether he is doing the right thing by listening to Successful Scott. After all, he really hasn't known him very long. And what about the path? What if Critical Craig was right and it doesn't lead to his bright new future? Average Joe begins to feel a little sick to his stomach. But after giving it some more thought, he decides that since he's already come this far, he might as well continue a little farther. Who knows, his bright new future may be just around the bend and he would hate to miss out on that.

A little ways down the path, Average Joe begins to feel better again and reassures himself that Critical Craig was probably just being critical as always. He was so involved in his own thoughts that he almost ran right into his father, Hard-working Hal, who was standing with his arms crossed in the middle of the path. Startled, Average Joe says, "Hi dad,

I'm..." but before he could finish his sentence, his father interrupts him and says, "Joe, I've already heard about this nonsense idea of yours about some bright new future. Now listen to me. I don't know what's gotten into you, but you've got a good job with a good company that pays you well and a family that depends on you. Trust me, nothing in this life comes easy. You've got to work hard and earn a living like the rest of us. You're mother is worried sick about you and the rest of the family thinks you've lost your marbles. It's time to quit this silly idea of yours and head back home."

Average Joe thought for a long time after talking with his father. He imagined what his family and friends were saying about him and became very discouraged. He realized that he must have been crazy to think that he could ever have a bright new future. After all, he was just Average Joe. Successful Scott must have been lucky. He probably had a really short and easy path; and anyway, he was born with the qualities of a successful person unlike Joe. And there really wasn't anything wrong with his life now was there? He makes more money than Laughing Larry and his family has food on the table and a roof over their heads. What was he thinking to change his whole life over some crazy idea?

And so Average Joe turned around and headed home. Never knowing what may have happened if he had continued on his path. And no matter how he tried to rationalize in his mind the reasons for turning back, he never quite settled the nagging in his heart that wondered what a bright new future might have been like for him.

What if we changed the ending for Average Joe? Maybe it would look something like this:

On the path back, Average Joe decides that he should at least go and see Successful Scott to let him know that he had decided to go home. After all, Successful Scott really had tried to help him. Successful Scott was happy to see Average Joe and invited him in for a cup of coffee. After listening intently to Average Joe explain all of his reasons for deciding to go home, he said, "Joe, it makes sense to me that you would want to go home. And I can also understand why Laughing Larry, Critical Craig, and Hard Working Hal feel the way they do. What's important is that

THE CURRENCY OF THE FUTURE

"Most people are too busy knocking opportunity to hear opportunity knock."
–Brad DeHaven

you're doing what's right for you. Joe, did I ever tell you what happened to me when I set off on my path to a bright new future?" Successful Scott went on to tell Average Joe about his journey and his own encounters with his good friend Negative Neil, his cousin Status Stan, and his father Sergeant Steel. "What I realized Joe, is that sometimes people are too busy knocking opportunity to hear opportunity knock. I thought everyone would see what I saw. And when they didn't, I was very discouraged and wanted, more than anything, to turn around and go home–many times. But thanks to a note that I had written to myself that I kept in my pocket, I persisted and eventually made it to my bright new future."

Average Joe was curious so he asked Successful Scott about the note. "I wrote it to remind myself of what was important to me and why. I read it to myself every time I became discouraged or doubtful, so much so that I memorized it and it became a part of me. Somehow, after reading my own words, I just couldn't bring myself to betray my own heart and turn back. Maybe you could write one like it Joe, so that you'll always know what's important to you and why you decided to pursue your bright new future." Average Joe thought about everything Successful Scott had said. He was surprised that it hadn't been a short and easy path for Successful Scott after all, and that he had faced his own doubts and critics just like Joe.

After a while, Average Joe thanked Successful Scott for his time and got up to leave. On his way out, Successful Scott said, "Joe, I believe in your dream and I know you can do something great with your life. I'm just a phone call away when you need to talk." With that, Average Joe headed off, amazed at how good he always felt after spending time with Successful Scott. A little ways away, he sat down, pulled out a piece of paper, and began to write down the things that he had carried in his heart for so long. When he was done, he folded the paper neatly, placed it in his pocket, and without hesitation, headed back out in the direction of the path to his bright new future.

Just like Average Joe, the criticism and doubts we face will be very real and discouraging. And our entire future often teeters on the edge as we decide who we will listen to. Understand that all opinions are not

101

created equal. If we're talking golf, Tiger Woods' opinion is going to count more than your neighbor's. If we're talking basketball, Michael Jordan's opinion holds more weight than your co-worker's. And if we're talking about your bright new future, the opinion of the person that has achieved theirs ought to outweigh the opinion of the person that has not.

Our belief initially can be sky high, but it is more likely based on sheer excitement rather than a deep rooted conviction. It certainly didn't take much for others to plant the seeds of doubt in Joe's mind during that time. Fortunately for him, he did the smart thing by taking advantage of the resources he had available to him–Successful Scott. He had valuable insight in what was unknown to Joe that helped him to protect and nurture his belief while it was still in its fragile state as well as help him learn a way to avoid future pitfalls that he may run into. While we may not all have a "Successful Scott" in our lives, we do have access to alternate resources that are just as viable, which we'll talk more about in the next chapter.

"The person who says that a thing cannot be done should not be interrupting the person who is doing it." –Chinese proverb

You Keep the F

When I left engineering to start a computer consulting business, I was criticized and doubted. Later, when I left my consulting business to start an i-commerce business I was ridiculed, questioned, and misunderstood. Most surprising to me was that my biggest critics were often family and friends. I couldn't understand why those closest to me wouldn't provide the most support. Have you ever watched a bucket of crabs? They all try to claw their way out of the bucket, but if any one of them gets ahead, the others drag it back down. Sadly enough, what happens to crabs can also happen with people.

When you decide to pull out of the pack, it often makes others uncomfortable. Because when you begin chasing your dream, it reveals those who are not. And people will react to you based upon how that makes them feel. Your greatest critics, though well intentioned, are mainly fueled by how your choices have made them feel, rather than by truth. By criticizing you, they are able to justify their own actions. Remember, people don't do things to you, they do things for their own reasons. Keep this in mind as you consider the hurtful comments that you may encounter in your journey to success.

"The man who is anybody and who does anything is surely going to be criticized, vilified, and misunderstood. That is part of the price for greatness, and every great man understands it; and understands, too, that it is no proof of greatness. The final proof of greatness lies in being able to endure continuously without resentment."
–Elbert Hubbard

Make a point to resolve in your mind once and for all that you will live what you believe. Once you have done this, respond to any criticism in a clear, calm, and assured way. Whatever you do, resist the temptation to react extremely. As much as we'd all love to temporarily drop our EQ and blast our critics, it's a waste of energy and also counterproductive. Revealing that their comments have triggered you will only invoke more of the same. Remain calm, steady, and unwavering in your beliefs, and hopefully your critics will lose interest. Or better yet, you'll prove them wrong!

"The greatest revenge is massive success." –Frank Sinatra

Here's a story of one young man who did just that. He was the son of an itinerant horse trainer who would go from stable to stable, race track to race track, farm to farm, and ranch to ranch training horses. As a result, the boy's high school career was continually interrupted. When he was a senior, he was asked to write a paper about what he wanted to be and do when he grew up.

That night, he wrote a seven-page paper describing his goal of someday owning a horse ranch. He wrote about his dream in great detail and he even drew a diagram of a 200-acre ranch, showing the location of all the buildings, the stables, and the track. Then he drew a detailed floor plan for a 4,000-square-foot house that would sit on the 200-acre dream ranch. He put his whole heart into the project and the next day he handed it in to his teacher. Two days later, he received his paper back. On the

103

front page was a large red F with a note that read, "See me after class."

The boy with the dream went to see the teacher after class and asked, "Why did I receive an F?" The teacher said, "This is an unrealistic dream for a young boy like you. You have no money. You come from an itinerant family. You have no resources. Owning a horse ranch requires a lot of money. You have to buy the land. You have to pay for the original breeding stock and later, you'll have to pay large stud fees. There's no way you could ever do it." Then the teacher added, "If you will rewrite this paper with a more realistic goal, I will reconsider your grade."

The boy went home and thought about it long and hard. He asked his father what he should do. His father said, "Look, son, you have to make up your own mind on this. However, I think it is a very important decision for you." Finally, after sitting with it for a week, the boy went to see his teacher and turned in the same paper, making no changes at all. He told his teacher, *"You keep the F and I'll keep my dream."*

Today, that young boy, Monty Roberts, now a grown man owns a 4,000-square-foot house in the middle of a 200-acre horse ranch. And he has that school paper framed over his fireplace. Two summers ago, that same school teacher brought 30 kids to camp out on his ranch for a week. When the teacher was leaving, he said, "Look, Monty, I can tell you this now. When I was your teacher, I was something of a dream stealer. During those years I stole a lot of kids' dreams. Fortunately, you had enough gumption not to give up on yours."

"Keep away from people who try to belittle your ambitions. Small people always do that, but the really great make you feel that you, too, can become great." –Mark Twain

Lighten Up!

Life is too short. Don't waste valuable time getting bent out of shape by what others think of you. Keep it in perspective. Sometimes all you need to take the pressure off is to find a little humor in the situation. I recently received the following e-mail newsletter from Brad Schell, Cofounder of an architectural design software company called SketchUp. Not only is his software program amazing, he has a great perspective. I love how he took something that could have ruined his day and had fun with it instead.

Fortunately, we get a lot of wonderful feedback, but that is not always the case. I have to share this one... it is so pure, so honest... it really made me smile.

"I'm writing to tell you that I hate your program. It is by far the most frustrating piece of software I have ever worked with, and I loathe it. So thank you for creating this horrible software, and making my day a living hell..."

I'd like to think writing that note might have kept the dog from being kicked, saved a computer or prevented the need for someone to sleep on the couch. So if you're really having a bad day or SketchUp has driven you to the brink, go ahead send me a flamer, let me have it, it is the least I can do....

"It is not the critic who counts: not the man who points out how the strong man stumbles or where the doer of deeds could have done better. The credit belongs to the man who is actually in the arena, whose face is marred by dust and sweat and blood, who strives valiantly, who errs and comes up short again and again, because there is no effort without error or shortcoming, but who knows the great enthusiasms, the great devotions, who spends himself for a worthy cause; who, at the best, knows, in the end, the triumph of high achievement, and who, at the worst, if he fails, at least he fails while daring greatly, so that his place shall never be with those cold and timid souls who knew neither victory nor defeat." –Theodore Roosevelt

Chapter IX
Never Stop Learning

My idea of "learning" through my college years was reading cliff notes, memorizing some facts, and putting them into short term memory for the test on Friday. It's no wonder I didn't read after college. I never felt that a book could have a profound impact on my life or the income I could earn. Then I heard a speaker at one of the very first seminars I attended say, "The books you read and the people you associate with determine your destiny." As I began wondering which of my college textbooks had any bearing on my destiny so far, the speaker rattled off the names of several books that I had never heard of. Books like, *How to Win Friends and Influence People*, *The Magic of Thinking Big*, *Think and Grow Rich,* and *Developing The Leader Within*. Now that I've read these books and countless others, I believe his statement hit the nail on the head.

While you don't have to make a huge financial investment to get started in The Currency of the Future, you do need to make an ongoing investment in your most important asset: YOURSELF. And here's a golden coin for your future: You don't live life as it is, you live life as you are. Imagine your driving experience on the open road in an outdated vehicle that hasn't been washed, checked, or fine-tuned for years. Assuming that you can even see through the windshield, how's your ride? Now compare that to the experience of driving in a completely reconditioned vehicle. Can you imagine the difference? The smoothness of the ride, the ability to feel and handle the road. Not only is the ride more reliable, it's enjoyable. Don't you just feel better driving an improved vehicle?

107

THE CURRENCY OF THE FUTURE

"You don't live life as it is, you live life as you are."

—Les Brown

Our mind, which contains our thoughts, perceptions, attitudes, and skills, is our vehicle through which we travel in life. Our experience on the road is only as good as our vehicle. What's more, the way others perceive and regard us on the road is also influenced by our vehicle. Improve your vehicle and you improve the ride. Ben Franklin said, "If a man empties his purse into his head, no man can take it away from him. An investment in knowledge always pays the best interest." Every top earner I know continually works on improving themselves; it's what gives them their edge.

I'm going to challenge you with a different kind of learning than what you may be used to. The kind of learning you used to do before you learned how to "learn." Young children, especially before the age of five, are highly *proactive* learners. As any parent will tell you, they're into everything! Exploring, trying, taking things apart, succeeding, and failing. They don't wait for anyone to "teach" them; they go for it! "Why?" is their burning question and their minds are continually processing what they learn from the endless world around them.

That's why so much of the truly important and difficult learning that people do happens so early in life. Children learn remarkably challenging skills like how to walk and speak a language with very little formal instruction. Their own desire to learn is the driving force. They learn without the prodding of teachers or the threat of a "test." They just dive in and do it! And they learn without being self-conscious or overly concerned about failure. That is proactive learning.

Unfortunately, most schools put the learner in the back seat and people are taught to become *reactive* learners. We're conditioned to react to the teacher and wait for them to tell us what, when, and how to learn. Sadly, much of the joy of learning withers away in the process and apathy sets in. Look in the window of a kindergarten class and watch the energy and movement. Listen to the children's genuine excitement and inquisitiveness when they ask questions. Compare that to a classroom full of adults, where in most cases, they have been trained to wait silently for instructions to learn. They react to the instructor, care more about their grade than what they learn, and stifle their questions for fear of "looking stupid." Their desire to seek out new information and skills is

THE CURRENCY OF THE FUTURE

"When your heart decides on a destination and believes that it is achievable, your mind proactively seeks to discover the way."

—Brad DeHaven

replaced by blank stares and frequent glances at the clock.

What is the difference? Is it our age? We've all heard the saying that you can't teach an old dog new tricks. Are we simply incapable? I don't buy that. The child-like learner can reappear in all of us. Several years ago, I had a friend who had a beautiful rock pool built in his backyard. As I watched the construction crew building synthetic boulders and rocks, I became utterly fascinated. As goofy as it sounds, it never occurred to me that anyone could just make rocks!

Several weeks later when I saw the resulting beauty complete with waterfalls and a slide, I knew I had to create my own rocks. The next day, I found myself studying pictures of rockscapes on the Internet and strolling around my property envisioning areas that could be enhanced with boulders, rocks, and a water feature. My creative juices were in overdrive and led to hours of childlike enthusiasm and fun as I researched, planned, and built my own rockscapes.

Once I saw that it was possible, I became proactive in achieving it. My mentor always said that the *will* to do, springs from the knowledge that you *can* do. Children have a strong desire to learn because they see the world as their playground; they haven't encountered enough "realists" to believe that there are limits to what they can do in life. Some people, on the other hand, have bought in to the fact that most everything, aside from a low paying job and a mediocre life, is impossible. Their disbelief is most often the result of never knowing or learning from anyone that has actually created wealth.

I remember growing up thinking, "The rich get richer." "The poor get poorer." "It takes money to make money." It wasn't until I began interacting with wealthy people that I realized many of them had very humble beginnings. Their money wasn't handed to them. They created it. The more I saw and the more I listened and learned from those who had developed their wealth, the more convinced I became that I could do the same. When the heart decides on a destination and believes that it is achievable, our mind proactively seeks to discover the way.

Timebinding

So why learn from others? Isn't it our own experience that is the greatest teacher? Absolutely! The mistakes we make are great teachers, but how fun are they? If I can save myself the aggravation of one mistake by learning from the experience of another, it's worth it. Utilizing the principle of *Timebinding*, we can save valuable time and effort by drawing from the compounded knowledge and experience of others. It allows an individual, a company, or an organization to produce far more in a shorter period of time than they would have been capable of had they started from scratch. When cell phones began incorporating digital cameras into their functionality, they didn't have to go back and re-invent the digital camera. And when HDTV was introduced, they didn't have to go back and re-invent the TV. With the use of timebinding, they were able to start where others had left off.

Timebinding is not limited to technology and the concept is nothing new. Einstein learned from Newton, Newton from Galileo. Martin Luther King read Ghandi; Ghandi learned from Tolstoy. Thomas Jefferson and Ben Franklin read John Locke, and on and on it goes. Writers read other great writers. Scientists build upon the discoveries of other scientists. Whether you are a business owner, a music composer, a football coach, or a parent, you can use timebinding to your advantage.

In fact, the book you are holding in your hands right now represents 10 years of reading self-development books and biographies, researching and collecting information, interviewing successful business owners, attending countless conferences, listening to hundreds of audios produced by some of worlds best teachers and motivators; and last but not least, learning from my own successes and failures. By reading through the thoughts contained within these pages and building upon them, you are exercising the concept of timebinding.

"Employ your time in improving yourself by other men's writings so that you shall come easily by what others have labored hard for."
–Socrates

The Price for Success

I was recently standing in line at a popular bookstore with a new friend. I had a book in my hand that I was waiting to pay for and my friend asked to look at it. He read the title, turned it over, looked at the price and said, "You are going to spend $39.95 for a book?" I responded by saying, "No, I'm going to spend $39.95 for a man's life. What took him 25 years to discover, I can learn in a few hours."

Average people don't understand the value of information. They look at the price tag and ask themselves, "Why is this so expensive? It doesn't cost that much to print this book or to duplicate this CD," as if its value existed only in its material composition. These people have obviously never experienced true learning.

The value of a book, CD, or any other information is in its ability to simplify and improve our lives. In Lance Armstrong's book, *It's Not About the Bike*, he writes about his journey back to life after being diagnosed with testicular cancer. For him, the value in learning was to save his life. "I became a student of cancer. I went to the biggest bookstore in Austin and bought everything there on the subject ... I was willing to consider any option, no matter how goofy ... I tore out pages of Discover magazine, and collected newspaper stories on far-off clinics and far-fetched cures." He became voracious for any information that might save his life. "I want everything. Everything, everything ... I wanted to know it all."

Since his journey back from cancer, Lance has won the Tours de France a record six times. Successful people live their lives with the belief that there is a solution to every challenge. They also believe that there is always more to learn.

What price are you willing to pay for the knowledge that can help you realize your dream? Let me ask the question this way: If I could provide you with the solution to a significant challenge that you're facing right now, whether in your career, your marriage, parenting, sports, or any other area of your life, what would it be worth to you?

Sometimes valuable information can be obtained for free, and there are other times when you might pay a hefty price for it. Realize that the greater the level of your challenge, the fewer the people who can provide the solution. And scarce resources typically cost more.

What if you invested $100 a month on information? Let's say you took the price of a frappuccino at Starbucks everyday and invested it into valuable information that increases your income. Would it be worth it? To spend $1,200 a year for information that would help you earn an extra $10,000 a year? Try that return in the stock market! What if it were to earn you $100,000 or $1,000,000 a year, but you thought it was too expensive so you spent it on the frappuccino instead? Talk about an expense!

The price for information may simply be cash out of your pocket, but it may also involve re-arranging an impossible schedule to be able to travel to another city and hear a speaker. Or maybe, the price entails waiting for hours to catch a moment with an important person to ask them a question. Whatever the price, your success depends on your ability to find and learn the information that paves the way for your dreams. Those who are unwilling to pay the price for success will never have the success they need to fund their dreams.

"Never let money separate you from wisdom." –unknown

I've heard it said that there are three kinds of information:
1. Things that you know
2. Things that you know you don't know
3. Things that you don't know that you don't know

The first category includes information that you know, like how to read a book, how to drive a car, how to balance a checkbook, etc. The second category includes things that you know you don't know. Some of the things that I know I don't know are, how to speak Spanish, how to fly a plane, Steve Jobs' cell phone number, etc. The last and most significant category includes all of the information that you don't know that you don't know. And this is where most, if not all, of the information you need to succeed will come from.

So, if you don't know that you don't know something, then how can you possibly learn what it is? You can start by figuring out who to learn from. All of your learning and knowledge up to this moment has brought you to where you are today. If you are not where you'd like to be in life, then it could be that you're not learning from the right people. Where does your knowledge come from? School, work, friends, the Internet, TV, radio, the newspaper? How much of that information comes directly from people who have accomplished what you are looking to accomplish in life?

There are top earners in your field who are publishing books, speaking, training, coaching, writing articles in magazines and E-zines, offering Webinars, and more. Seek out resources from those who have earned their success doing what you are trying to do. While you can certainly learn a great deal from someone who has crossed a mine field, you'd be better off learning from someone who has been through the exact mine field you're trying to cross.

Once you find the right source, form a daily habit to absorb the information and apply what you learn. Learning isn't some momentous event that only happens during a scheduled semester. Rather, it is an ongoing process, a habit that is developed through our daily actions. Could you listen to a CD during your commute time in the car, or while you're preparing a meal? Could you carry a book with you and read from it during those wait times at the doctor's office or at the car wash? A Gallup poll found that high-income people read an average of 19 books per year. That compares to 1.9 books per year in the general population; a 10-fold difference! Successful people find creative ways to cram valuable learning time into their hectic, busy lives. They may only have 10 or 15 minutes a day to read a book or listen to an audio CD, and they may not necessarily be the fastest learners, but they are consistent learners and that is what keeps them on top of their game.

Association

I've heard it said that in 5 years your income will be the average of your five best friends. I thought, "Wow, I need to find some new friends!" Funny, but so true. The fact is, how you spend your time and who you hang around with determines your future. Association with people more

THE CURRENCY OF THE FUTURE

"Most people sleepwalk through life.
They just do enough to get by and
meld into the unhappy masses.
If 'All the world's a stage,' too
many people are content
to play the audience."
—unknown

excellent than ourselves challenges and guides us in our own experience. It is a significant component in our journey to success.

At a recent business conference, I was speaking with an affluent business owner in the automobile industry. I knew his family and asked him how his two high school boys were doing. He mentioned that Rich, his oldest son, wanted to go into the investment and money management field. He went on to explain how he hired a top financial advisor and CEO of a large brokerage firm to mentor his son. Once again, I learned that successful people think different. Any "logical" parent would have sent their son to a leading scholastic institution to get an expensive education.

Think about it: What are the chances of Rich landing a great position with a prestigious firm after being mentored by the "Warren Buffett" of his industry? Rich has learned current and proven street smarts in his field by sitting in board rooms with experts, answering phone calls, and conversing with millionaires. He didn't study text books, he studied the top earner in his field. How does that compare to a top college graduate with an expensive education on dated theories? It's common sense that's not so common.

Most likely, you won't have the privilege of being personally mentored by a top producer in your field right off the bat. You can, however, begin to seek and associate with those that have had more success than you in what you are attempting to accomplish. If you're like me, you weren't brought up around cocktail parties for the rich and famous. So how does an average citizen increase the level of their association?

Start by meeting and connecting with people outside of your usual routine. What are your interests and experiences? Find networks and associations in those areas and attend their events with the intention of meeting and talking with people. You never know who will play a key role in developing your Currency of the Future.

Choose your friends and associates wisely. Be aware that we typically feel most comfortable around people at our own level of thinking. If you're comfortable around your friends who are filling your ears with bad news, gossip, and complaining, I have one simple answer for you. "Find new friends!" Challenge yourself to link up with bigger thinkers. Average minds tend to talk about people and events. "Did you watch the game last night?" "Can you believe what Shelly said to Julie?" Big minds mainly talk about ideas and vision. Here are some statements I hear from my "bigger thinking" friends:

"What did you learn from that mistake?"
"Have you read this book on leadership?"
"I've researched a business opportunity that can pay a great return in 10 years."
"What are your goals for this year?"
"How can we help people accomplish more?"

Start hanging around people who think big. Don't make the mistake of associating with people based on your comfort and ease around them. The right associations and mentors will stretch your thinking, guide you out of your "comfort zone," and focus on leading you to success rather than being your buddy.

In the movie *Jerry McGuire,* there's a scene where Jerry becomes fed up with his client Rod's attitude and pleads, "Help me help you!" Help your mentors and associates help you. People prefer to help those who want to be helped. Are you teachable? Do you complain and blame, or do you take responsibility? Do you find yourself arguing your point rather than listening to, and considering their advice? Are you appreciative and respectful of the time and opportunity others offer you, or do you take it for granted? Are you open to considering perspectives you initially disagree with, or do you just shut down? Do you make it easy for others to get along with you and express their thoughts? Help others help you by being someone who they can, and want to help.

A friend recently came to me for some advice on how to drum up some more business. He insisted that he was doing everything right, but for some reason his growth had stagnated. I knew him well and knew that he had a tendency to want to be right about everything. So long as he made his point, in his mind, he was doing everything right. Unfortunately for him, it was limiting his ability to effectively work with people. When I asked him what his associates thought and how they felt about things, he became defensive and replied, "Well, I told them...." No matter how I tried, he just wasn't willing to hear the advice. I suggested several books, which he has read with no improved results. He had plateaued, and until he was willing to learn and change, my advice wouldn't matter.

"When the student is ready, the teacher will appear." –Zen proverb

The most important advice is often the hardest pill to swallow. I'll be the first to admit, I hate finding out that I'm the problem, that me, myself and I are what is standing in my way of progress. And when we are face to face with our ego, we'll either set it aside for the sake of progress and face our own hard truths, or we'll take the easy road and continue to ignore it or discredit the source. When we take the easy road, we plateau in our capacity to learn. And no matter how favorable our circumstances may be, our income will never exceed our willingness to change and grow.

Do you want to know where the money is in your business? Here's the secret: It's where you don't want to go and where you aren't willing to grow. It's where your fear is, where your struggles are, where you refuse to change. I like to say, "No change, no chance!"

The most hazardous obstacle in your journey is to think that you have already learned everything there is to learn in any area of your life. Our learning process is just that–a process. Can you remember a time when you visited an old familiar place, maybe a childhood home or a school you attended a long time ago? I remember once going back and visiting the home I grew up in to see if it was still there. As I pulled up to the house, there was a familiarity about it, but I was stunned by how small it seemed compared to how I remembered it. What I realized was that the house hadn't shrunk, I had grown up and my perspective had changed. The process of learning is very much like that experience I had.

When you were a teenager, weren't you convinced that you knew more about life than your parents did? What happened when you "grew up" and maybe got married or had children of your own? Did your perspective change? Did you start to think that they may actually know a thing or two after all? What we learn and what we're capable of seeing changes as our perspective grows through our experiences in life.

We should never feel like we've "arrived" in our learning, nor should we be discouraged by comparing ourselves to people who are more skilled and seasoned than ourselves. It's easy to look at someone who's accomplished and think that they've just "had it" all along. What you don't see is the "before" picture: the unrefined original, the countless hours they invested learning, and their awkward attempts at what seems so effortless to them now. Instead of measuring yourself to a master, measure your success and growth from your own starting point.

"It's what you learn after you think you know everything that makes all the difference." –John Wooden

Be a Champ

Sometimes I associate with others to learn and challenge my thinking, and sometimes I associate just to be around other great men and women who are also in the trenches pursuing their very best life. It's sort of like a safe haven from the wears and tears of the road, where there is a shared understanding of the experiences we face along the way. I am truly grateful for the privilege I have of being able to associate with these champions in my life.

My wife and I have done our best over the years to instill an "attitude of gratitude" in our kids. One day I came home to find my seven-year-old son Blake at home lying on the couch. I asked Kim, "Did school end early today?" and she said "No. He has a high fever and was sent home." I walked over to Blake and felt his head. I could see that he looked terrible so I asked him, "How ya feelin' champ?" And without missing a beat he said, "Great." His response was a bit muffled, but he's learned that the only answer to the question, "How are you?" is "Great." In fact, all three of our children have only one answer to that question. It's not "Fine," "Good," or "Okay." It's "Great!" Well, for our four-year-old it's "Gate!" He's still working on his R's.

The American Dream

When you understand that there are children dying in the hospital, being sent home from school sick truly is "Great." And when you understand what a privilege it is to be able to learn freely, you will. You don't *have* to learn, you *get* to learn. You get to chase your dream. They say that foreigners who come to the United States are four times more likely to succeed than those who are born here. Why? Because they value the freedom that so many Americans take for granted. They come here with a dream in their heart and build their own businesses, while most Americans live as if they are slaves to their boss.

Recently, I was eating lunch with a friend I hadn't seen in over a year. As we were exchanging updates on our lives, he mentioned to me that he was sending his son, Eric, to live in Mexico for a year once school was finished. I thought it unusual, so I asked him, "Why?" His reply was revealing. "I grew up in a small fishing village in Mexico where I worked 6 days a week for our family to get by. We didn't have much and every day was a struggle, but we were grateful for what we had because we knew there were families that had no work, no place to live, and no food to feed their children."

"I used to dream of coming to the United States where my family would have the chance for a better life. It seems that most people who are born here don't value any of it. Americans are more interested in entertainment: American Idol, computer games, and Internet trash. I'm sending Eric to Mexico so that he'll learn to cherish America's true greatness."

Curious, I asked, "So what's that?" He replied, "It's the American Dream. The opportunity to get off of the bench and onto the playing field, to sweat and strive, to chase your dreams, and to have the chance to live an extraordinary life."

This country needs more champions–people who are willing to step up and live their dream, to do what is uncomfortable and inconvenient to become extraordinary. Great men and women gave their lives and paid a price so that you would have the freedom to live yours. They sacrificed so that you would have the chance to do something great with your life. *Will you?*

THE CURRENCY OF THE FUTURE

"We don't have a clue as to what people's limits are. All the tests, stopwatches, and finish lines in the world can't measure human potential.

When someone is pursuing their dream, they'll go far beyond what seems to be their limitations. The potential that exists within us is limitless and largely untapped. When you think of limits, you create them."
—Robert Kriegel

Chapter X
Ignite!

Theodore Roosevelt once confessed, "There is nothing brilliant nor outstanding in my record, except perhaps this one thing: I do the things that I believe ought to be done... And when I make up my mind to do a thing, I act." No matter how much you learn from the principles in this book or how great a business idea you may have your hands on, without action, they are utterly useless. Friends, this is where the rubber meets the road. Talk is cheap. Your time is not. If you want to build a successful business, start building.

I can remember when my brother-in-law and I were brainstorming about business ideas back in 1996. We came up with a concept that combined a coffee shop with Internet connections at all the tables. It would have coffee, snacks, a web connection, and the services of Kinko's all in one. "We'll call it Tek-Java!" I explained with excitement. Everyone will want to hang out there. We'll franchise the idea and make millions!

I thought about it for years... until many others came along and actually did it. Starbucks, for one, has made a fortune of it. Others took action while I idled, and the difference is of drastic proportions. I heard that it wasn't the guy who discovered electricity who made all the money, but the guy who set up all the meters. An idea, in and of itself, has no intrinsic value. It must be accomplished by action. The successful implementation of one good idea is worth more than a thousand great ideas never acted upon. Thus, the phrase, "Ideas are a dime a dozen."

"You miss 100 percent of the shots you don't take." –Wayne Gretzky

When a rocket leaves the launch pad, it uses 95 percent of its energy in the first three minutes! It's the initial push that is needed to breakthrough. In his book, *The Art Of The Start*, Guy Kawaski describes time-tested, battle-hardened advice for anyone starting anything. He says, "The hardest thing about getting started is getting started. Remember: No one ever achieved success by *planning* for gold." His advice: Forget mission statements and business plans, they're long, boring, and irrelevant. No one can ever remember them–much less implement them. Start creating and delivering your product or service. In essence, "Put Microsoft Word, Excel, and Powerpoint aside, and get on the phone, talk to people, build a prototype, write software–whatever it is that your business requires to start generating income."

I once had a business partner who was always enamored with projections. He would produce beautiful spreadsheets and presentations predicting huge profits. On one particular day, he shared with me his latest profit spreadsheet regarding an exciting new product. He eagerly pointed to the screen of his notebook computer and said, "If we move just 100 cases, watch how the bar chart changes. Isn't that awesome?!" To which I responded, "Yeah, that's great–but you're still broke."

All of business ultimately relies on sales. Without it, there is no business. Guy Kawaski puts it this way: "You should always be selling– not strategizing about selling. Don't test, test, test–that's a game for big companies. Don't worry about being embarrassed. Don't wait to develop the perfect product or service ... It's not how great you start–it's how great you end up."

The valuable time wasted by people contemplating the "what if's" of business must be as massive as the black hole that sucks up missing socks. No matter how you look at it, it's still theory and no one will ever know what will happen until someone goes out and actually does it. Observe the Noah principle: You don't get a prize for predicting the rain. You get the prize for building the ark.

If you act, then fail, at least you learn what not to do in the future and

THE CURRENCY OF THE FUTURE

"Tenacity is more than endurance, it is endurance combined with the absolute certainty that what we are looking for is going to transpire. Tenacity is more than hanging on, which may be but the weakness of being too afraid to fall off. Tenacity is the supreme effort of a man refusing to believe that his hero is going to be conquered."

–Oswald Chambers

move ahead with increased knowledge. With inaction, the only thing you learn is theory and the fact that you didn't act.

Pleasure and Pain

Every action we take in life is based on an underlying desire to either seek pleasure or avoid pain. A person who is overweight may commit to watching what they eat to avoid the pain associated with being overweight. But what happens when they go to a friend's dinner party where they are served a piece of rich, savory cheesecake? An internal struggle arises between the pleasure of eating the cheesecake and the desire to avoid the pain of being overweight. Whichever desire is perceived to be greater and more imminent in their mind will prevail.

Is your desire to achieve your dream substantial enough to prevail when you're tired, tested, discouraged, and uncertain? Will it measure up to the other desires you face, like wanting to relax, please others, take time off, or even quit? Your dream should not be some fuzzy idea that you think of once a month. It must be reinforced daily if it's going to influence your decisions daily. Think about your dream and what pleasure it will bring you when you achieve it. Is it comfort, accomplishment, security, recognition, virtue, or something else? Whatever that pleasure is for you, picture yourself living it. Imagine yourself fulfilled by it and how that will make you feel.

On the other end of the spectrum, we can protect ourselves from inactivity by enhancing our desire to avoid pain. If achieving your dream in your mind is about recognition, then your most profitable pain factor is its adverse–embarrassment. Now find ways to reinforce the connection between your activity and the avoidance of that pain in your daily life. One way to do this is to set up some form of accountability for yourself or with a partner. Decide on a consequence that will cause you this exact pain if you fail to accomplish your daily, weekly, or monthly goals and have someone help you follow through.

One of my associates' Achilles' heel was watching television. Try as he may, he always gravitated back to this damaging habit, wasting hours of productive time. His wife was pregnant at the time with their first child and I remembered how his eyes filled with delight as he excitedly showed me the picture of their unborn child from her first ultrasound. His dream was to replace his wife's income so that she could stay home and raise their child while he comfortably provided a great lifestyle for his growing family.

Later, when he asked me what he could do to replace his habit, I suggested that he take the ultrasound picture of his unborn child, blow it up, and paste it to his television screen. That way, every time he looked at the television, he would be reminded that his action was tied to his wife's ability to raise their unborn child. To watch TV, he would literally have to set his child aside. As you can imagine, watching TV wasn't very comfortable for him anymore.

One of my more memorable consequences was agreeing to shave my head if I failed to meet my action goals. There was absolutely no way I was going to be caught dead without my helmet and I can remember looking at myself in the mirror every day fearing what I might look like without any hair. Talk about motivating! Thankfully, I never did have to shave my head.

I only tell you that story as an example, not a recommendation. Accountability is not for everyone and it is definitely not to be imposed on others. The desire to win and discipline ourselves to action must come from within. The essence of leadership is embracing people where they are, empowering them to be more, and equipping them to prosper.

I heard a story about an old man who was sitting on his porch with his dog. A bystander couldn't help but notice them because the dog had been groaning in pain for quite some time. He walked up to the old man who hadn't seemed to take much notice of his dog's suffering and asked him, "Why is your dog groaning?" To which the old man replied, "He's lying on a nail." "Why doesn't he move?" The old man answered, "Because it doesn't hurt bad enough."

Like that dog, most people are groaning about their quality of life, their low pay, lack of job security, and mushrooming personal debt, yet they aren't doing a thing about it. When that rusty nail gets sharp enough, perhaps from a layoff, an unexpected illness, a bankruptcy, or simply

THE CURRENCY OF THE FUTURE

"Every day men fail morally, spiritually, relationally, and financially; not because they do not want to succeed, but because they have blind spots and weak spots which they surmise they can handle on their own. One of the greatest reasons men get into trouble is that they do not have to answer to anyone for their lives."

–Patrick Morley

because they've reached the tipping point of an unfulfilled life, people will begin jumping to action. Don't wait for a nightmare. A big enough reason today will cure any inactivity.

"And the day came when the risk to remain tight in a bud was more painful than the risk it took to blossom." –Anais Nin

Overcoming Action Jammers

In the following section, I have come up with a few suggestions that will help you take the next step to overcoming some of the common action jammers people face along the way.

Most of us want to, and already have an idea of how to improve our lives, yet very few are actually willing to do it. Why? Are people really just lazy? I believe that there is more to it than that. I believe they are uninspired. They drag themselves to work so they can earn their paycheck to get them through another month, another year. Their work is demanding, yet unfulfilling and meaningless to them. There is nothing fueling their efforts and at the end of the day, they come home completely exhausted thinking, "I hate this, but I just don't have the time or energy to do anything else."

What these people fail to realize is that when they find their passion and purpose in life, and when they discover a way to perform work that is meaningful to them, there is boundless energy. An entire reservoir of vigor and vitality springs forth within them from the belief that they truly are making a difference and affecting their future. Their business, their work, and their family life are all impacted by the hope and excitement of chasing their dream. People aren't lazy; they are uninspired and unaware of what matters to them. They simply haven't found their purpose in life.

How do you find your purpose? Mike Murdock says, "What infuriates you the most is a clue to your future." What do you get angry about? For example, if "politics" and a lack of integrity in your office angers you, your purpose may be to build or create a business based upon sound leadership and integrity. If poverty in your downtown streets angers you, your purpose may be to earn or organize the funds to make a difference in your community. If what your children are learning in school upsets you, your purpose may be to find a way to improve their education and the education of children all across the country.

Actively spend an hour or two on the weekend writing down ways that you could use your gifts and creativity to generate income doing what inspires you. It is imperative for you to always write your thoughts down on paper. In doing so, you will gain clarity and your ideas will go from random obscure thoughts to distinct possibilities. Don't limit your creativity by thinking about logistics. This is simply an exercise of ideas, not implementation. Imagine that anything is possible. What could you do? What would you love to do? What would be the ideal way for you to make a difference while earning a great living?

With any idea or opportunity, stop saying, "I can't." Investigate instead. Look below the surface and see if you can find purpose and meaning first. Then ask yourself this question: Does it matter to you? Remember, reasons come first, answers come second.

Another reason people choose not to improve their lives is because they are afraid to venture into the unknown. They want to change, but their current situation is familiar to them and there is comfort and security in that. Attempting to change is different and it involves variables that they don't understand, so they resist it. It's like the soldier who was captured by the enemy and given a choice: He could either take a bullet to the head or exit through a door at the back of the room to face an unknown fate. For fear of what may lie behind the door and the possibility of a gruesome death, he chose the bullet. What actually awaited him behind the door was his freedom, but he never got to see it because he was unwilling to act and take the risk.

Instead of always sticking to what is familiar, make a new habit of doing what is unfamiliar to ease you out of your "familiar zone." Try a new coffee, get a new hair style, take off to a new place for the weekend, drive a new route to work, try a new recipe, try a Mac computer instead of an IBM, make a new friend, or fly a new airline. What you will learn from these experiences is that the unknown can be great, and it can be bad–but you'll never know until you actually do it!

"*People in distress will sometimes prefer a problem that is familiar to a solution that is not.*" –Neil Postman

Fear of failure and fear of rejection are two more prevalent causes for inactivity. Both of these fears shift our focus off of the greater purpose behind our actions and onto our own troubled selves. It is a process of inflating the "what if's" to unrealistic proportions. Do not allow yourself to vividly imagine what you don't want to happen. Instead, picture what you do want to happen. Remember, what is programmed into our auto-pilot (subconscious mind) steers our course.

Ask yourself this question: Have you ever stepped out and done something that was new or uncomfortable? Have you ever started a new job or moved to a new town? Do you remember the fears you had about that particular activity? What happened to those fears? Did they become a reality? If you answered yes, then ask yourself, have things somehow worked themselves out since then? Are you still alive and kicking?

What these fears come down to is this one question: "Do I have what it takes to succeed?" I remember asking myself that very question years ago, and I still ask it today. Part of me wants to shy away in fear, yet there's another part of me that feels like John Wayne, the rugged cowboy emerging from my core. The fact is, the answer to that question has little predictive power regarding what you'll actually do when you get caught up in a powerful dream. None of us will ever know if we have what it takes until we actually do it.

Unfortunately, you're not going to find a recipe to "overcoming your fear in 21 easy steps" in this book, because there is no such thing that will eliminate all of your fears. Everyone has them. We wouldn't be human otherwise. But not everyone allows their fears to stop them. I still get butterflies doing the things that I have practiced for years; the difference is that I've trained them to fly in formation. Realize that taking action does not require the absence of fear, it requires acting in spite of the fear. Some people invest more time and energy trying to figure out a way to produce results without having to face their fears than they do actually facing them! As Nike says, "Just do it." Fear and all, *just do it!*

131

One of the most insidious obstacles to taking action is procrastination, which occurs as a result of some of the fears we've already discussed, and also from a lack of focus on the right priorities. In Chapter III, we covered the Achievement Cycle: Dream, Goal, Plan, and Effort. Your priority is your Dream, and all Goals, Plans, and Efforts must be with that end in mind. If your actions and efforts are mainly in areas that are not contributing to your dream, you are procrastinating.

If you're waiting for everything to be just right before taking action, you might as well wait 'til your 6 feet under the ground. Let's face it, your calendar will never clear up, things will never be under control, the urgent will always attempt to distract the important, and things will never "settle down." Welcome to life. Things have a tendency not to happen. You have to make them happen. Let me bring you back to the lyrics of an old classic song...

A child arrived just the other day,
He came to the world in the usual way.
But there were planes to catch, and bills to pay.
He learned to walk while I was away.
And he was talking 'fore I knew it, and as he grew,
He'd say, "I'm gonna be like you, dad.
You know I'm gonna be like you."
And the cat's in the cradle and the silver spoon,
Little boy blue and the man in the moon.
"When you coming home, dad?" "I don't know when,
But we'll get together then.
You know we'll have a good time then."
My son turned ten just the other day.
He said, "Thanks for the ball, dad, come on let's play.
Can you teach me to throw?" I said, "Not today,
I got a lot to do." He said, "That's ok."
And he walked away, but his smile never dimmed,
Said, "I'm gonna be like him, yeah.
You know I'm gonna be like him."
And the cat's in the cradle and the silver spoon,
Little boy blue and the man in the moon.
"When you coming home, dad?" "I don't know when,
But we'll get together then.
You know we'll have a good time then."

Well, he came from college just the other day,
So much like a man I just had to say,
"Son, I'm proud of you. Can you sit for a while?"
He shook his head, and he said with a smile,
"What I'd really like, dad, is to borrow the car keys.
See you later. Can I have them please?"
And the cat's in the cradle and the silver spoon,
Little boy blue and the man in the moon.
"When you coming home, son?" "I don't know when,
But we'll get together then, dad.
You know we'll have a good time then."
I've long since retired and my son's moved away.
I called him up just the other day.
I said, "I'd like to see you if you don't mind."
He said, "I'd love to, dad, if I could find the time.
You see, my new job's a hassle, and the kid's got the flu,
But it's sure nice talking to you, dad.
It's been sure nice talking to you."
And as I hung up the phone, it occurred to me,
He'd grown up just like me.
My boy was just like me.
And the cat's in the cradle and the silver spoon,
Little boy blue and the man in the moon.
"When you coming home, son?" "I don't know when,
But we'll get together then, dad.
You know we'll have a good time then."
–Cat's in the Cradle, lyrics by Harry Chapin

We often think that just because we are busy, we are productive. Nothing could be further from the truth. Busyness is the worst possible excuse for an unrealized dream! You should never be too busy to think about and prioritize what matters most in your life. If you haven't done it already, take a moment and figure out your Achievement Cycle. Now take what you have written down for "Effort" and schedule that into your calendar first. Next, look at everything else that you add to your calendar and ask yourself, "Why am I doing this?" If you can't find a convincing reason, it does not belong in your calendar!

Brian Tracy, a great proponent of "thinking and acting strategically," in his book *Eat That Frog!* states that the key to reaching high levels of performance and productivity is to develop the lifelong habit of tackling your biggest, hardest, and most important task first thing each morning. Develop the routine of "eating your frog" first. Do not procrastinate and leave your frog on your plate to stare at all day. It will continue to distract you and you'll feel green by the time you have to eat it! Instead, launch directly into your tasks and then work with single-minded focus until they are complete.

"The things that matter most must never be at the mercy of the things that matter least." –Johann Wolfgang Von Goethe

The ridiculous truth about both traffic jams and action jammers is that we create them. There is no accident or obstruction in the road up ahead. It's just a row of vehicles all hitting their brakes out of unnecessary fear and confusion.

One of the ways I trick myself into getting more done is to play little mind games with myself. I withhold my simple daily pleasures until I've completed a set task. For example, I love my coffee and after I've made myself a fresh cup, I won't allow myself to indulge the first sip until I've dialed the phone number to my next important call. If I'm hungry, I'll finish what I'm working on before I grab a bite to eat. By playing these little games, not only do I accomplish more, I also perform my tasks with greater urgency. As silly as it may sound, I am accomplishing a little more every day, which over the course of time amounts to a significant increase in my overall productivity.

A common misconception people have about action oriented people is that they're just naturally motivated all the time. The truth of the matter is that no one is *always* motivated. Some just choose to be more disciplined than others. Motion precedes emotion. The "feeling" to act does not descend upon us out of the blue. Don't just sit around waiting for a surge of inspiration–act your way into a feeling instead. When you act, the emotion will follow. Conversely, when you stagnate, your emotions deteriorate. As discussed in Chapter II, Emotional Intelligence will play a significant role in your success. To consistently take action over long periods of time, you will eventually have to come to terms with the fact that you're going to have to conquer your emotion of not

134

wanting to act.

If you know you're feeling unmotivated, stay away from areas that may cause you to stagnate–the break room, the kitchen, sometimes even your office can be a trap with its piles of paperwork and overflowing inbox. Instead, grab your cell phone and a notepad and go for a walk to make your calls. If your work doesn't involve making calls, go for a 5 minute run around the block to get your blood flowing. Change your pace, change your scenery; do something to change your state of mind. An old Chinese proverb says, "Man standing on mountain with mouth wide open waiting for roast duck to fly in has long wait." They were wrong. Man actually died of starvation. If you want it, you have to go and hunt it.

"The first and greatest victory is to conquer yourself; to be conquered by yourself is of all things most shameful and vile." –Plato

THE CURRENCY OF THE FUTURE

"Whether you're a mom wanting to earn a little income, a disenfranchised employee wanting out of the rat race, an aging adult concerned about retirement, whatever your reason... you can find or build a vehicle to achieve your dream."

Chapter XI
Find Your Vehicle

Whether you're a mom wanting to earn a little income, a disenfranchised employee wanting out of the rat race, an aging adult concerned about retirement, whatever your reason... you can find or build a vehicle to achieve your dream. The question is, how do you know what is the right vehicle for you?

While I can't answer that question for you, perhaps I can guide you in the right direction. In this chapter, we'll discuss ten powerful characteristics that I believe constitute the design of an ideal business. Although the business you decide to build may not incorporate all ten, my goal is that you will find some ideas and gain valuable insight that will put you in the driver's seat of the vehicle that is right for you. Let's look at those ten characteristics together:

1. Low start up cost
One of the biggest reasons why more people aren't starting their own businesses is that it typically costs a lot of money. Operating a traditional business involves many fixed costs like a storefront, utilities, stocked shelves, and staff just to mention a few. These fixed costs are a "stress monster" for most traditional business owners because they are paid whether you are open for business or not.

Today, however, many of these costs are no longer a deterrent because anyone can start and operate a business right out of their own home. The Internet is rapidly becoming the new marketplace where the storefront and office is replaced by an online website, and products can be made to order. Moreover, those who operate a business from their home are able to enjoy the many tax benefits that go along with it. They can "write-off" many of their expenses like a portion of their mortgage payment, phone bill, utilities, and many others that would otherwise be money down the drain every month. You work hard enough for your money. Why shouldn't you keep more of it?

Turn-key business models providing people with the opportunity to start and operate their own business with minimal costs will continue to grow in demand as more and more people become aware of the benefits. Additionally, businesses that provide products and services that enhance the efficiency and capacity of these new online businesses will also profit and thrive in the years to come.

2. Offers items that are in high demand

What do toothpaste, cell phones, vitamins, cosmetics, razor blades, coffee, diapers, insurance, and dog food all have in common? People need them and will continue to buy them whether the economy is good or bad. They are great products to build a business on because they are basic items that most everyone will want or need to buy. What other products and services can you think of that fit this description?

Wayne Gretzky became known as the "Great One" in hockey for his ability to skate to where the puck was going, not where it already was. In business, we profit based on our ability to "skate" to where the money is going, not to where it already is. If you haven't been successful yet, you may have missed some trends. If you want to build a strong business that can lead to financial independence, you need to invest in what is *going* to happen, rather than what has *already* happened. For example, if you were the best at manufacturing cassette tapes, would it matter today? Of course not, it doesn't matter how great your product is when it is in an eroding industry. CDs, MP3 players, and fixed disc recording devices are what people will want and need in the future.

Let's take a look at the trends and what is going to happen. One major area of interest that analysts have watched for years is the advancement of the population born between 1946 and 1964 known as the "baby boomers." This generation accounts for some 76 million people in the US alone and 1 billion people worldwide. As this post World War II generation has made their way through the stages of life, they have been compared to a watermelon making its way through a garden hose! Predict what a billion people are going to want or need to buy and you can make a fortune.

What do a billion babies need? Baby food, right? Well, Gerber sold 2 billion jars of baby food by 1955! How about shoes and toys? Buster Brown, Kinney, Mattel, and Hasbro became wealthy providing shoes and toys to this group! As these baby boomers grew older and began buying homes starting in 1975, we saw the largest real estate boom in history. They also proved capable of negatively impacting industries when in the early eighties, their buying trend began to wane and the real estate boom fell through the floor. Homebuyers were drying up, but the homebuilders kept on building causing a surplus as well as many bankrupt businesses in that industry.

Over the next 10 to 15 years, the real estate industry will be hit by the back end of this cycle. You can expect to see some hot home deals when those same baby boomers entering into their retirement years begin cashing out their larger expensive homes downgrading to condos and retirement communities instead. These are just a few examples of how some industries win or lose based on the buying habits of this group.

Now let's move to the present. You have a billion people between the ages of 41 - 59. What business do you want to be in? What are some of the obvious trends we can predict? What does an aging population want and need? How about a vacation! The tourism and vacation industry will experience significant growth as this generation moves into their retirement years. How about health and wellness, looking younger, feeling better, retirement needs, and efficiencies that simplify life? In his book titled, *The Next Trillion*, Paul Pilzer outlines the biggest consumer tidal wave to ever hit this country. You guessed it–the health and wellness industry. Why? Because, baby boomer or not, we all want to look great and live longer.

Now consider how this aging population will purchase the things they are going to buy? What would be the easiest, most efficient way for them to access these goods and services? Will they continue to drive to the store, push their carts up and down the aisles, and carry heavy packages? Perhaps, but more likely, a friend or relative will show them how simple it is to buy it online and have it conveniently delivered to their door.

Harry S. Dent, in his book, *The Roaring 2000's,* predicts that the peak spending years of baby boomers along with the explosion of e-commerce will combine to create the biggest economic boom in the history of the world! Furthermore, Frank Feather, author of *Future Consumer.com* states that "By 2010, the Internet will gobble up 31% of consumer spending, leaving most brick-and-mortar retailers in rubble." He goes on to say that, "The head-spinning Internet Revolution, or 'Webolution,' will reverse virtually everything the Industrial Revolution put into place, returning the workplace, the learning space, and the marketplace, back to the home. This webolution will rock your world, utterly transforming life and commerce. And its rewards will accrue fastest to those who embrace it first."

3. Offers items that have repeat purchase

What could be better than owning a business that sells products and services that people want and need? How about owning a business that sells products and services that people want and need over, and over, and over again? My mentor once asked me this question: "Which would you rather have, 10 percent of all the BMW's or 10 percent of all the coffee sold in the U.S.?" I laughed and replied, "I may be young, but I'm not stupid–the BMW's of course!" From the look on his face, it was apparent I chose the wrong answer.

Although BMW's, Jacuzzi tubs, and corporate jets are all very sexy and have a much higher ticket price and net profit per unit sold, not everyone buys one, and even fewer buy one every year. BMW sells approximately $10 billion worth of cars in North America. Compare that to the $20 billion of coffee consumed in the U.S. annually.

Companies like Proctor & Gamble, Johnson & Johnson, and Kraft understand the power of repeat purchases. They have remained profitable giants in the business world for years by selling the items we all use, day in and day out. Whoever invented Drāno was a genius. Think about it: People go to the store, buy it, take it home, and pour it down their drain. Then they go back and buy more! Get the idea?

4. Distributes rather than manufactures (be an agent)

Here's a little story that will give you some perspective on the manufacturing opportunities in America today:

> Joe Smith started the day early having set his alarm clock (MADE IN JAPAN) for 6 a.m. While his coffeepot (MADE IN CHINA) was perking, he shaved with his electric razor (MADE IN HONG KONG). He put on a dress shirt (MADE IN SRI LANKA), designer jeans (MADE IN SINGAPORE), and tennis shoes (MADE IN KOREA). After cooking his breakfast in his new electric skillet (MADE IN INDIA), he sat down with his calculator (MADE IN MEXICO) to see how much he could spend today. After setting his watch (MADE IN TAIWAN) to the radio (MADE IN INDIA), he got in his car (MADE IN GERMANY) and continued his search for a good paying AMERICAN JOB. At the end of yet another discouraging and fruitless day, Joe decided to relax for a while. He put on his sandals (MADE IN BRAZIL), poured himself a glass of wine (MADE IN FRANCE), and turned on his TV (MADE IN INDONESIA), and then wondered why he can't find a good paying job in... AMERICA.

A funny story, but at the same time shows the ignorance of many. The Industrial Age is over! Joe Smith will probably never find a good paying job in America manufacturing anything. Joe Smith needs to turn off his TV (MADE IN MALAYSIA) and read this book (MADE IN AMERICA)!

The best opportunities today do not exist in manufacturing, but rather in distribution. The faster technology races along the faster products become obsolete. Why would you want to invest in the manufacturing equipment

THE CURRENCY OF THE FUTURE

"The head-spinning Internet Revolution, or 'Webolution,' will reverse virtually everything the Industrial Revolution put into place, returning the workplace, the learning space, and the marketplace, back to the home."

–Frank Feather

to make CDs when they will be tomorrow's eight-track tape?

In today's economy, 70 to 80 percent of the cost of most retail products is in distribution. Even if you were the best and most efficient company manufacturing CDs, your profit margin would be miniscule compared to its distribution profits. This also explains why the world's greatest individual fortunes between 1970 and 2000 were amassed by people focused on distributing things rather than making them.

Even the industry of distribution is evolving, from the physical distribution of products themselves to the intellectual distribution of information about them. Sam Walton (Wal-Mart) became the richest man in the world in 1991 by physically distributing to customers what they already knew they wanted. By 1999, Jeff Bezos (Amazon.com) became *Time* magazine's "Man-of-the-Year" by teaching customers about products that they didn't even know existed. Intellectual distribution is the wave of the future. It is evident in the emerging wellness industry, in the distribution of technology and information (Google, Yahoo), and other areas where the majority of future customers do not yet know that the products or services even exist.

5. Can eventually run without you

As mentioned earlier, the key to creating wealth is to create something significant and make yourself an insignificant part of it. If your goal is financial freedom, you will never attain it by continuing to create income in the "time for money" trap. It doesn't matter whether you make $10 an hour or $1,000 an hour because the day you stop working is the day you stop getting paid. If your income is dependent on your ability to perform–to get paid forever, plan on working forever.

The advantage of a "system" run business is its predictability. This includes: affiliate programs on the web, prosumer arrangements, network marketing businesses, and franchising. The franchisor (or mentor) says to the franchisee (or business owner), "Let me show you how it works." And work it does; the system runs the business and the people run the system. The system integrates all the elements required to make a business work and transforms it into a machine.

Today, there are many businesses that can offer the advantages of franchising through the implementation of a proven system. Many large companies have affiliate programs or prosumer arrangements that allow you to create business for them, and in return, they share their profits with you. By affiliating with a large company, you have the ability to instantly tap into a business that's already organized, powerful, and successful. You immediately gain access to the advantages of a large company without all the headaches and financial risks involved.

6. Has the ability to leverage to others (duplicate)

The ability to leverage your business to others is the missing link for those who are trying to become financially free in a self-employed business. This concept can best be described by first understanding what "leveraging" is all about. Remember Kiyosaki's "CASHFLOW Quadrant" from Chapter II? As an Employee or a Self-employed person, you exchange your time and expertise for money. The problem with this is that if you're not exchanging your expertise, you're not making money.

A logical solution might be to get more education to raise your wages, but you are still limited by time. True wealth is beyond anyone's reach without the use of leverage. On the right side of the quadrant, the Business owner and the Investor generate income by leveraging their resources. They know that true wealth is created by either people at work or money at work.

Money at work looks like this: Lets say you have $5 million earning a 10% return. It will yield approximately $500,000 per year or a little over $40,000 a month in income. You're leveraging your money and your money is working for you.

People at work looks like this: Suppose you own a company and you have one employee named "Ed" who works an 8-hour day with you. You get paid for 16 hours of work because you take a portion of Ed's productivity for your company. You are leveraging off of Ed's effort because Ed is your employee. So theoretically, the more employees you have, the more leverage you have.

But is hiring more employees really the right solution to increasing your leverage? If you've owned a company with employees before, you know that in theory it's a great way to achieve leverage, but in reality, it's very difficult to accomplish. The reason is simple: No employee will ever work as hard for your company as you do because they don't own it. Remember the rented car example? They don't own it, so they won't wax it! For you to have "true leverage" you must create a situation where everyone has the same amount to gain.

Another problem with leveraging yourself in a traditional business is that employees, salespeople, artists, contractors, and agents alike are all limited in their ability to leverage themselves the way that you as a business owner can. This creates a conflict until they do what most business owners dread–they leave your affiliation with everything they learned from you and go start their own business. You not only lose them as an income source, they are also now your competitor!

Who trained this new competitor? You did! They know exactly how you run your business and all of your trade secrets. It happens in practically every industry. Have you ever heard the expression, "I'm just working there for the experience."? What they mean is, I'm going to strip them of their knowledge, then go do it myself. Now fast-forward the clock a few years. What happens to the people they hire who have limited leverage? They do the same thing and the cycle goes on and on.

In network style businesses, everyone has the same opportunity to leverage themselves. Not only that, the more leaders you train and develop who leverage themselves, the more profit you both earn. There is no incentive for them to break off from you to start over because they are already in the ideal leveraging position. This system gives you the incentive to do everything in your power to help your leaders learn and grow. Trying to hold them back or not showing them all of your best marketing methods is cutting your own throat. It also makes sense for you to help the people your leaders are training because you are financially rewarded for it. So it's a win/win situation for everyone involved. The only way you or I can ever retain a true leader is to provide them with the same opportunity for growth that we have.

Some people see this and say, "Isn't that a pyramid?" Well, what does that mean—a pyramid? It's not the geometric shape that people question. Your family tree is the shape of a pyramid, so is the government and practically every other business or organization in the world. To the architect, it is the strongest structure known to man. Most people that ask this question really mean that it's structured so that the people at the top get all the money and the people at the bottom do all the work.

Well, what about the typical corporation? Isn't there a CEO at the top of the chain? Does an area manager, for example, earn more money than the CEO? Of course not. Do any of the office clerks earn more money than the area manager? No. There is a chain of command and each level of the corporate structure earns less income.

Even in occupations such as sales where a company may claim there is no ceiling, we see those who have had their commission restructured to insure their income remains proportionately below that of the company executives. Within a corporation, the people at the top make most of the money and the people at the bottom do not. That's what I call a "pyramid."

I think it would be a mistake for anyone to dismiss direct selling (multi-level marketing) as a viable way to create financial freedom. Robert Kiyosaki calls these opportunities a "personal franchise" for the average person. It gives the *little guy* a chance to build a *big business*. The fact is, the industry has matured enough in recent years to be worth your time to investigate. Anyone who remembers the old days of Avon, Mary Kay, or Shaklee will be shocked when they take a new look. What used to be considered Mickey-Mouse opportunities are now web-savvy, multinational, multibillion-dollar giants that have earned noticeable rank in the business world.

Don't take my word for it. Look at it from an investor's point of view. Warren Buffett, one of the world's richest men and a highly respected financial guru recently invested in a direct sales business. He obviously believes that an industry approaching $100 billion a year is worth capitalizing on.

146

With network marketing, you have the very same opportunity as anyone else. Its structure is fluid in that it allows for a person to make as much or more than anyone else. The income you earn is based on the volume that flows through the number and size of organizations you build. In other words, you get paid for what you produce. The more profit you bring to the organization, the more profit you keep. Now that's "fair." Free enterprise at its finest in my opinion.

Despite the fact that these network style businesses have been misunderstood, companies like Microsoft, Sony, Disney, Nabisco, Office Max, IBM, Circuit City, Levi's, and hundreds of others continue to link up and distribute their products through this channel. These affiliations are a firm testament to the industry's growing success and credibility.

Think about why it's a good business decision for any corporation to distribute their product through a referral-based system. Traditionally, for a business to get their product into the market they would first have to spend a fortune on advertising to create awareness. Then they would have to hire corporate reps or distributors to move the product into the market, all of which adds to the company's cost of selling the product. Before a single product has ever been sold, just to get it on the store shelf, it trades hands several times and gets marked up in price so that each business involved along the way also covers their costs and makes a profit.

Do you think companies like having their products marked up in price? Of course not. They're not in business to make money for middlemen. They're in business to make money for themselves. Many businesses are racking their brains trying to figure out better and more efficient ways to distribute their products so that they can increase their profits while maintaining a competitive selling price. Cut the middlemen, increase profits. And what better tool than the Internet to provide the solution.

Another way to increase profits is to maximize advertising efforts. Typically businesses spend upwards of 20 percent of their budgets advertising their products through TV, radio, billboards, banner ads, etc. I heard one CEO of a large corporation tell his board members, "Half of our advertising dollars go to waste. The problem is, we don't know which half." Businesses that affiliate with referral-based systems have the ability to instantly tap into a loyal consumer base that does all of the advertising for them. When, and only when their product is sold do they pay advertising dollars for the referral. This unique solution makes for 100 percent effective advertising. Smart business? Absolutely. It is the best kept secret in marketing today and that is why more and more companies are joining these smart channels of distribution.

7. Access to a successful mentor
There is a lot of merit to the phrase "In business for yourself, but not by yourself." One of the biggest reasons people never venture into the Business owner quadrant, or even the Self-employed quadrant is because of their fear of the unknown. Years ago, when I was working at a computer supply business, I did exactly what we talked about earlier. I took everything I learned in that business and started my own.

What I soon realized was that the information I thought to learn before starting my business wasn't nearly enough. Many questions and concerns arose that I had never anticipated before opening my doors for business. For obvious reasons, I couldn't go back to my previous employer to get his advice on the challenges I was facing. In fact, anyone that had the knowledge and experience I was seeking would have considered me their competition. Left to my own devices, I ended up in quite a hole.

That experience taught me an expensive lesson on the importance of following in the path of a successful mentor. I wasn't one of these "self-help" junkies who bathed themselves in the latest success book or seminar. I didn't need motivation, I needed direction and focus; I didn't need a coach on the sidelines, I needed a mentor in the trenches with me; I didn't need a one-size-fits-all rah-rah message to motivate me for the moment, I needed a custom designed system that would keep me inspired and profitable for a lifetime.

To achieve greatness in business and in life, we all need a mentor, a guide, a counselor, someone to "show us the ropes" to success. Ideally, it is someone we can trust who has a vested interest in our financial success; someone who sees our potential, regardless of our past who will lead us to live it.

A well-known speaker once started off his seminar by holding up a $20 bill. He asked the room of 200 people, "Who would like this $20 bill?" Hands started going up around the room and he continued, "I am going to give this $20 to one of you, but first, let me do this." He proceeded to crumple up the $20 dollar bill. He then asked, "Who still wants it?" Still the hands were up in the air.

"Well," he replied, "what if I do this?" And he dropped it on the ground and started to grind it into the floor with his shoe. He picked it up, now crumpled and dirty and said, "Now, who still wants it?" Still the hands went into the air.

The lesson was this: "My friends, we have all learned a very valuable lesson from this $20 bill. No matter what I did to it, you still wanted it because it did not decrease in value. It was still worth $20."

Many of us have been dropped, crumpled, and ground into the dirt by the decisions we have made and the circumstances that have come our way. And though we may feel worthless at times, no matter what has happened or what will happen, you will never lose your value. Dirty or clean, crumpled or finely creased, you are still priceless to those who love you and believe in you.

"The chief want in a person's life is to have someone help them to do what they know they can do." –Ralph Waldo Emerson

8. Make a life, not a living

John's daughter asks, "Can you read me another story?" "I'll read you a different story tomorrow. You have to wake up early for school and the clock says it's time for sleep." After a prayer of thanks and an exchage of kisses, John heads downstairs to the kitchen where he fills his mug with some freshly brewed coffee. He makes his way back to his favorite leather chair in his home office and turns on his video camera peering off his 23-inch flat panel display. He checks his e-mail one last time before the video conference begins and hopes that no news is good news.

A moment later John's computer chimes and Chuck's face appears on his screen. "Hi John, is that your first or second cup of joe tonight?" "It's my first." John replies as he sips from his mug. "I just put the kids to bed. By the way, what's the weather like in Beijing?" "It's a gorgeous morning. How are things in Chicago?" "Beautiful, and it'll be even better if you liked the packaging artwork I sent you last Friday."

Seem distant, far off, or futuristic? Hardly. John's scenario is a sign of the times.

People today are looking for ways that work and family can be mutually reinforcing parts of an integrated life, and technology is making it all possible. 72 percent of workers say they would work fewer hours–if only they could find a way to do so.

The business owners who apply technology and creativity along with some "elbow grease" will position themselves in the midst of what my mentor calls the "Perfect Storm": the Internet revolution, the peak spending years of the baby boomers, and the emergence of a home-based workforce.

In 1956, William Whyte wrote a book titled, *The Organization Man.* At that time, "The Organization Man" marched into our vocabulary and had a profound social impact. The label described what was then the quintessence of work in America: An individual, mostly male, who ignored or buried his own identity and goals in service to a large organization, which rewarded his self-denial with a regular paycheck, the promise of job security, and a fixed place in the world.

The Organization Men often preached rugged individualism, but instead of living by it, Whyte states that they lowered "their sights to achieve a good job with adequate pay, proper pension, and a nice house in a pleasant community populated with people as nearly like themselves as possible."

Today, we are seeing the antithesis of The Organization Man. In his book, *Free Agent Nation*, Daniel Pink writes, "Consider this: Fewer than one in ten Americans now works for a Fortune 500 company. The largest

THE
CURRENCY OF THE
FUTURE

"America's new icon will be the independent 'Free Agent' –the tech-savvy, creative, adventurous, path-charting entrepreneur."

–Brad DeHaven

private employer in the U.S. is not Detroit's General Motors or Ford, or even Seattle's Microsoft or Amazon.com, but Milwaukee's Manpower Inc., a temp agency with more than 1,100 offices in the U.S."

Men and women alike, empowered by the increased efficiencies of the web and new technological devices, either have already or are looking to break free from the chains of a large company to become agents in control of their own future. America's new icon will be the independent "Free Agent"–the tech-savvy, creative, adventurous, path-charting entrepreneur. More and more people are becoming disillusioned at having to climb through an organization and instead, are looking to create their own life on their own terms.

USA Today reported that the average commute time is 52 minutes each way. That's almost an extra two hours per day–an extra 10 hours per week! That adds up to 500 hours, or 12 work weeks per year. In 10 years, that equals 2 years just commuting! How many of those people do you think would enjoy commuting to work in their underwear?

eBay is one of the newest genres in the growing home-based business industry. The company was started by Pierre Omidyar in 1995 and as of April 2004, boasts more than 100 million registered users–nearly half of which have bid for, bought, or listed something in the previous year. It is estimated that eBay provides a marketing platform for some 450,000 Internet entrepreneurs who individually gross anywhere from $100 to $1 million a month.

According to Frank Feather, somebody new starts a home-based business every 11 seconds–that's 50,000 a week! Of those who already own home businesses, 81 percent say they like the freedom and having control over their own destiny. Making money actually was a motivator for less than 50 percent of them. But a whopping 93 percent say they have no regrets and that they would do it all over again.

It is no surprise that home-managed businesses are cropping up in cities and towns across the nation faster than ever. The News is filled with disturbing stories and statistics about the economy, stock market, mergers, outsourcing, corporate fraud, business bankruptcies,

THE CURRENCY OF THE FUTURE

"I didn't choose to enter this life, but now that I'm here, I have a responsibility to do something with it."

–Brad DeHaven

downsizing, and more. People are looking for ways to turn "home sweet home" into an income producing office.

There are over 20 million home-based businesses in the U.S. today generating an estimated $450 billion a year in revenues. And one out of every six working adults in the U.S. is connected with a home-based business, more than half of them on a part-time basis. Before you decide to dismiss these as some little "mom and pop" operations, take a look at the facts: *Money Magazine* reported that one out of every five home-based businesses produces an annual gross income of $100,000 to $500,000! And the Small Business Administration reported that nearly 20,000 entrepreneurs have already grossed more than $1 million a year operating their businesses from home.

In the past, home-based businesses may have been viewed as a hobby or a secondary source of income, but the revolution in information technology has given rise to the home as a hub of business activity and entrepreneurship. The way we work in America today is transforming rapidly and those who cater to this new business sector will grow and thrive in the years to come.

9. You can use your gifts and passions

One of the greatest aspects of building an exceptional team in any business is that the leadership that evolves is truly the cream of the crop. I couldn't have hand picked a finer group of individuals who are living The Currency of The Future. There is a natural selection process that occurs when leadership is tested, and those who rise up to the occasion are those that choose to live their best life.

"Love what you're doing. Believe in your product. Select good people."
–Debbi Fields

Not one of us chooses to enter this life, that's God's decision. But now that we are here, we have a responsibility to do something with the life that we've been given. We are all uniquely equipped with gifts that only we can develop and apply. Whatever your vehicle, do something great with your life. Don't get to the end and give yours back unopened.

10. You can be recognized

Recognition is by far, the most undervalued practice and the best kept secret in business and in life today. People grow and flourish in an arena where they are recognized for every small step that they take. It fosters job satisfaction, builds self-esteem, and reinforces desired performance. It also promotes trust, respect, and exceptional teamwork.

Our ignorance to this most important principle can be shaped by a belief that recognition is a touchy-feely, warm-fuzzy thing that only women connect with, or that it is only valuable in competitive sales environments. If this is your belief, you are missing the boat on the most powerful motivating force you possess in working with others. It is the best kept secret in business and in life. Try it, and you will see people who have not responded to anything else crawl over broken glass for sincere praise and recognition. The most precious gift we can offer others is our sincere praise and encouragement. We may not all admit it, but everyone craves it!

And before you gloss over this paragraph, THINK about what I said... It's the best kept secret in business and in life! That means not only in the workplace, but also in your community and at home. Friends, neighbors, associates, bosses, employees, preachers, teachers, leaders, parents, children, brothers, and sisters all respond to sincere praise and encouragement. The following story illustrates the impact of one mother's encouragement in her son's life.

> *When I was three years old my father passed away, leaving my mother alone to teach four boys how to grow and live and love. It wasn't easy for her at all; she worked twelve hour shifts as a teacher who taught night school. But somehow she managed to pull it off. She would come home late, fix us dinner, listen to our stories, and put us all to bed before she had any time to herself. We never thought much of it at the time, but it's obvious now that we were her life. I remember asking her about it, why she made so many sacrifices for us, and her answer was amazing.*

> *"Your success will be my greatest achievement."*

THE CURRENCY OF THE FUTURE

"In business, we profit based on our ability to 'skate' to where the money is going, not to where it already is."
–Brad DeHaven

From that day on my attitude and actions changed. I had the strength and the courage to deal with problems instead of turning away. I wanted to push myself to new heights and racing towards this challenge was the answer. She came to every competition and was always the first person at the finish line and the last person to leave. I can still hear those words that changed my life. Her goal was to give us a leg up and the opportunity to do great things, my ambition is to take that opportunity and run with it.

"There are high spots in all of our lives and most of them have come about through encouragement from someone else. I don't care how great, how famous or successful a man or woman may be, each hungers for applause." –George M. Adams

Perhaps like me, you have become both a victim and a contributor to the ignorance of this vital principle. Here is a two-question survey from author Eric Harvey that makes the point.

1. *Do you ever feel unappreciated or under recognized for the good you do?*
2. *Do you ever miss opportunities to recognize the people you work with for the good work that they do?*

If you're like most of us, there's a good chance your two answers were DUH! And OOPS! (i.e., yes and yes).

I love to tell the story of my wife when she was called in for jury duty. As she took her seat in the courtroom among the other prospective jurors, the bailiff began introducing the presiding judge. After all of his credentials had been stated and the judge was introduced to the jury, Kim began to applaud him. Her applause drew everyone's attention in the otherwise silent courtroom. Somewhat embarrassed by the fact that she was the only one clapping, she chuckled to herself realizing that she was in a different environment than what she had grown so accustomed to. You can bet that she was that judge's favorite juror that day.

"There is more hunger for love and appreciation in this world than for bread." –Mother Teresa

THE CURRENCY OF THE FUTURE

The Design of an Ideal Business:

1. Low start-up cost
2. Offers items that are in high demand
3. Offers items that have repeat purchase
4. Distributes rather than manufactures
5. Can eventually run without you
6. Has the ability to leverage to others
7. Access to a successful mentor
8. Make a life, not a living
9. You can use your gifts
10. You can be recognized

The Currency Of The Future

Chapter XII
The Payoff

Though my journey has only just begun, everything I have given up and sacrificed along the way has been worth it for what my family and I have gained in return: for my freedom and for the deepened friendship and love with my beautiful wife who has always made me feel like a hero, for the precious time I have been able to invest with my children, for the lives that we've touched, the friends we've made, and for the wild adventure it has been. If I had to start all over, I would do it again in a heartbeat, to earn my freedom and have the chance to create the life I choose to live.

Had I known back then what I know now, it would have been a much easier road. There were moments when the road seemed to cave in on me from every direction and I wondered if the price was worth it. The following is an entry from my journal during one of those times:

The past few years have been bittersweet. I have been blessed, but I have struggled. I have remained hopeful, but at times I have lost hope. I have made mistakes, but I have been forgiven. I have been sidetracked for moments, but I have remained reliable and trustworthy. I've taken hits and wondered if it is worth it to keep on. But I have remained on the field and I've stayed in the "front row." Regardless of what has happened or how I have felt, I have never left "the game."

It's a new day and I will step into it. I will remain in the "front row." More than anything, I need to become the man that God wants me to become. I will not despair, I will not get weak in heart, and I will never give up!

Wherever I see a seed of ambition, I will water it.
Wherever I see an embryo of leadership, I will nurture it.
Wherever I see the smallest spark of hope in someone's eyes, I will fan it, and bring it to a flame.

I was made for this, gifted for this, and I will be held accountable for this. Do this and you will hear, "Well done my good and faithful servant."

Will your journey be worth it for you? Only you can know the answer to that question when you get there. Maybe you'll think it was worth it when you earn your freedom and you walk out of your boss' office for the very last time knowing that tomorrow, and all the days for the rest of your life, belong to you.

"Money doesn't buy happiness but it sure can give you the giggles."
–Brad DeHaven

Maybe you'll think it was worth it as you and your family excitedly pack and prepare for that long awaited vacation you always talked about taking. Or, when you wake up for the very first time in your new home and lay there for a moment, just to let it all sink in. Maybe it'll be worth it as you adjust the driver's seat in your brand new vehicle exploring all the gadgets and features before driving off to have lunch at your favorite restaurant. Maybe it'll be worth it just to see that look of love and respect in your spouse's eyes, or for the peace of mind knowing that your family is financially secure.

Maybe it'll all have been worth it to see the tears of relief in an aging relative's eyes as you tell them not to worry, that you're going to take care of everything; or to receive a phone call from your church telling you about the lives they have impacted because of your faithful contributions. Maybe it'll be worth it as you seal an envelope full of cash anonymously addressed to a family in need.

Maybe it'll be worth it to see your parents swell with pride as they mention you to their friends; or to see that priceless look of surprise followed by a hint of embarrassment as you bump into old friends who doubted your chances at success. Or maybe, it'll be worth it when you look in the mirror and for the first time in your life, you see a person who is truly living the life they dreamed of. Only you will know at that moment, if it was worth it for you.

I love what Dawna Markova said in her book, *I Will Not Die an Unlived Life*. "I need to shed, to let go of what no longer is alive, to get bare enough to find the bones of what is important to me. I need to let go of the ways of knowing that have not, cannot, and will not take me where I want to go." *Will you let go and live your dream?*

Martin Baxbaum wrote: "You can use most any measure when you're speaking of success. You can measure it in a fancy home, or an expensive car or dress. But the measure of your real success is one you cannot spend–it's the way your child describes you when talking to a friend."

Is your life a proud reflection of who you are? What would those who know you best, truthfully, say about you? While I can't predict the words my children would choose to describe me, I hope it would go something like this:

My dad is the best! He loves me lots and tells me I'm special and that I can do great things in life.

He's a hard worker, but always takes time to throw the football or play with me.

When I meet his friends, they talk about possibilities, places to go, things to accomplish, and people they can help.

Sometimes we go out and look at things, big things.

THE
CURRENCY OF THE
FUTURE

"My dad says his purpose is to
set an example. He says, 'People don't
listen to the words you say, they watch
your actions of the day.'"

—Blake DeHaven

My dad never says we can't afford something. He says, "Well, we'll just have to help more people."

My dad wants everyone to win. He tells me to "Think big!" and says that I can have anything I want if I help enough people get what they want.

Sometimes he has me work in his office, or out in the yard. He always says, "Work before play."

I think my dad really has a crush on my mom because he's always trying to impress her. Besides that, he's always sneaking her li'l kisses and tickles. I think my mom likes that stuff a lot.

My dad says his purpose is to set an example. He says, "People don't listen to the words you say, they watch your actions of the day."

When I grow up, I want to be just like my dad.

When It's All Said and Done

Life is short, life is precious, and life will end for all of us. My personal belief is that we will all be accountable for how we choose to live the one life that is given to us. I believe there will come a day when you will meet your creator. I've imagined that day might go something like this: God meets you at the entrance to your next life. But before taking you through, he sits you down and shows you the moments of your life as you lived them. As you watch and relive your past experiences and actions with Him, you are at times embarrassed, ashamed at some, but laugh and smile at others. When it is done, you think, "I could have done so much more, I could have done so much better."

He then shows you another life. Again, it is you, but with bittersweet eyes you gaze upon the life that "could have" been. You watch the golden opportunities that were placed into your life that convert to abundant and fulfilling rewards. Sure, you saw setbacks and challenges, but in this life you used them as stepping stones to greatness. You lived your dream. Your life was a masterpiece.

Whatever your beliefs may be, make your life a masterpiece. Don't get so caught up in trying to make ends meet that you miss out on making a life. Don't allow your trivial busyness to keep you from enjoying life's most precious and satisfying seasons. The overtime hours, softball leagues, and Saturdays spent waxing your classic car will all be meaningless in the end.

None of us get a second chance. We have only one brief moment in time, one chance, to either live our very best life, or regret... wishing for what could have been.

The Alchemist, Paulo Coelho, says the world's greatest lie is this: "That at a certain point in our lives, we lose control of what's happening to us, and our lives become controlled by fate. That's the world's greatest lie."

Your life is not controlled by fate; your life is controlled by you. *You can live your dream.* It's your choice; it is in your hands.

I want to end my life with "no regrets." No regrets.

I hope that through our journey together in this book, I've challenged you to revisit the course of your life: to discover your dream, identify your obstacles, and chart new paths to forge ahead. And perhaps, for the first time, you've challenged yourself to really *think*.

I believe that "an obstacle identified, is half overcome." When you close this book in a moment and have a clear idea of the obstacles you're ready to overcome, the circumstances you're ready to change, and the dream you're ready to chase, YOU'RE HALFWAY HOME! You're halfway home to living the life you were designed for. Live your dream. Go for it! The Currency of the Future is waiting for you.

THE CURRENCY OF THE FUTURE

"Life is not a journey to the grave with the intention of arriving safely in a pretty and well preserved body, but rather sliding in sideways, thoroughly used up, totally worn out and proclaiming, 'Wow! What a ride!'"

–unknown